A Heart Frozen in the Wilderness

The Reflections of a Siberian Missionary

Mary Kloska

En Route Books and Media, LLC
St. Louis, MO

ENROUTE
Make the time

En Route Books and Media, LLC

5705 Rhodes Avenue

St. Louis, MO 63109

Cover credit: Sebastian Mahfood with image design by
Mary Kloska

Copyright © 2021 Mary Kloska

ISBN-13: 978-1-952464-81-2

Library of Congress Control Number: 2021939130

Table of Contents

Foreword

The icon on the cover of this book is of the Holy Family in a Siberian forest. Jesus is the center of the icon—and you can see that even as an Infant, He is the 'Savior.' His Hands and Heart are pierced open with nails and wounds—lifted towards those gazing upon Him in a sign of Fiat surrender to the Father's will, as well as in a sign of blessing. The way that light encircles Him reminds the onlooker that His Infant presence is a Eucharistic Presence.

Here you see Jesus as the 'shoot sprouting from the stump of Jesse.' He is the little flower bud opening upon the world to shed His Light, Grace, and Fragrance upon all. Our Lady's clothing represents the Divine Love of the Holy Spirit filling Her. St. Joseph's green and brown clothing represent how he was Jesus' earthly Father and Guardian. Both Mary and Joseph have flowers coming from the base of their clothing. Mary's are red with the passion—Joseph's are purple with the passion, yet hidden more in darkness as he is left so much of a mystery in Scripture. And you see this great Love of Our Lady (consumed by the Holy Spirit) and the Love of St. Joseph (hidden in earthly realities) come together to encircle the Christ Child. He is both God and Man.

I completed this book on May 1, 2021—the Feast of St. Joseph the Worker. This is something that was arranged by Providence, for this Feast Day was created in the Church by Pope Pius XII in 1955 to combat the Russian Communist holiday of 'May Day' (celebrated as a 'day of work.') It is also fitting to note that most of my missionary work done in Russia was in the 'Diocese of St. Joseph in Irkutsk.'

Except for my short high school experience in Moscow and a short stint in Vladivostok, the bulk of my time in Russia was in this Diocese named after our patron today.

As I note in the final chapter, in Fatima Our Lady asked for all to pray for the conversion of Russia and She reassured us that when this did finally take place, that the Triumph of Her Immaculate Heart would happen in the world. And so this book will be published May 13, 2021— the anniversary of the first apparition of Our Lady to the children in Fatima. In all of this we see how important the Holy Family is in the plan of God for the Russian people.

For all of these reasons, this book is dedicated to St. Joseph, Mary, and Jesus—particularly to St. Joseph, the Worker, Our Lady of Fatima and the mystery of the Christ Child-Savior, truly present in the Eucharist. I also dedicate this book to the millions upon millions of Christians martyred by Stalin and the Communist regime for their faith. It is dedicated to the tireless, selfless missionaries who have offered both sweat (work) and love (grace) in their service of the Russian people as they try to rekindle and strengthen their faith. And it is dedicated to my beloved Russian friends as well—it is to you that Our Lady looks as the chosen ones to usher in the Triumph and Reign of Her Immaculate Heart.

Come Holy Spirit!

Mary, Fiat. +

I write this book as a cry for help,
as Jesus' cry of *"I thirst"* on the Cross.
Russia needs missionaries.
Russia needs prayer.
Russia needs Love.

(St. Seraphim of Serov, Pray for us!)

Chapter 1

A Seed in the Heart of a Child

One day when I was in the third grade my dad took me into his bedroom and opened up his 'treasure box'. Buried on the bottom of this little wooden box was a real Russian penny (really it was a ruble) that a relative of his had taken off of a Russian soldier who had died in World War II. Placing it in my hand, he told me that I could take it to school for 'show and tell,' yet he reminded me that it was a real treasure and that I had to be careful with it. I wrapped the penny up in tissue, put it in a baggy and cautiously tucked it into my pocket. Somehow, my heart was lit afire just knowing that it was from Russia (although I did not know why that made me so excited). I showed the class in the morning, and then I put the penny back into my desk. But at the end of the day, it was gone. Now I realize that someone must have stolen it, but at the time that thought never crossed my innocent mind. I thought that I had lost it, and I was extremely sad for my father—I cried and cried. I searched my lunch bag that had been thrown into the trash. I searched everywhere. I was so afraid to tell him that I had lost it, for it was his treasure. I remember that feeling of helplessness—I did not know how to replace such a treasure. And the fact that I had lost it remained as a weight around my neck for years (I am not exaggerating, I often thought of it and would feel guilty again). I remember my guilt only being relieved when I finally was able to go to Russia myself, and I could bring my father back many Russian pennies. He, of course, was never that upset about losing it. But my conscience felt like I owed him some sort of recompense. It is interesting for me as I reflect back on my life how God used this little incident with a Russian penny in the third grade to plant a missionary seed in my heart. For it was through losing that silly, little ruble that God began to build a desire in me to go to Russia— simply so that I could bring my father back another 'Russian penny' to replace the one I had lost. I knew very little about Russia, but from that young age I began to be interested in her and to love her.

From the time I had been very little, I had been told to "Pray for the conversion of Russia." It had also been explained to me that in Russia people were not free—the government controlled everything in their lives down to deciding a person's profession for them. And worst of all, I had heard that in Russia they were not even allowed to believe in God. After school one day, when I was in grade school, I remember being surprised when cartoons were interrupted with a newsbreak showing the tearing down of the

Berlin Wall. I did not, even when I eventually was in high school, understand all the implications of what had happened in the former Soviet Communist-run countries, yet I knew that it was serious. Nor could I ever have dreamed that a future priest friend's father was the head of the KGB in East Germany when Communism toppled and that a priestly vocation was being born hidden in the heart of a KGB officer's son. I just prayed—and somehow God was already uniting hearts. I did not know or care if it was dangerous in Russia. I really wanted to visit them, simply to love Jesus among them.

Chapter 2

The Gift of Love is a Responsibility...

"It was not you who chose Me, but I who chose you...to go and bear fruit that will remain..." (John 15:16)

My First Summer Mission Trip to Russia in 1994

One Wednesday evening in February of my junior year in high school when I attended our weekly Medjugorje rosary prayer group at my friends' house, Jesus had a great surprise waiting for me there. Towards the back of this family's big prayer room sat a few little sisters dressed all in white. As I began speaking with them, I came to learn that they were from a newly formed community in Slovakia. They spoke to us that night of their community's new mission in Russia and the upcoming Summer Russian Mission trips. My heart jumped as I heard them say "Russia". And I felt a strong pull in my heart as these sisters began to speak about it. I felt very strongly that Jesus somehow wanted for me to go there. I did not think, *"Oh, I want to go and preach the Gospel and convert Russia!"* Instead, the thought that echoed loudly in my 17-year-old heart was, *"I must go and love Jesus for them, and love them for Jesus!"* After our prayer meeting, I approached one of the sisters, who mentioned that they sometimes allowed lay volunteers to join them in their summer's work. I asked if I was too young, or if maybe there would be a possibility that they would allow me to join them as well. There was another young girl at the meeting, who was a year younger than I, and she also was interested in going. This sister said that she would speak to their community's head priest and find out for us.

A few weeks later I received a letter in the mail from that sister saying that it would be possible for us to join them, encouraging us in our desire and providing the information that we needed to arrange travel. Although that one big obstacle was overcome (receiving permission from the head of their community), many more laid before me as I still needed to receive permission from my parents and also somehow come up with the more than $1,000 I needed for a plane ticket. Yet Jesus had His plan, and He opened all the doors before me with His grace. My parents agreed to let me go, providing that I myself earned the money for my ticket. To this day they do not know why they agreed, for their minds were full of reasons as to why they should have forbidden me to go—including that I was too young and that Russia had only recently been freed from dangerous, Communist Rule. Yet, Jesus' grace overrode all and they simply said yes. I began to save up all my money from my work after school at a little gift shop, from my work in the evenings with abused children and from extra babysitting. In the end, I would be about $300 short, and my parents helped me out by lending me the

TRAIN RIDE TO moscow

money with the under-standing that I would pay them back as I received my paychecks the following year. I remember the great excitement in my heart when after all this had fallen into place for me, my new friend from our prayer group (who also wanted to go to Russia) called me and left a message that her parents, too, had given her permission.

I did not know at all what to expect out of the summer that lay before me. I am embarrassed to think now that I had packed two suitcases—one big one and one small one—for my short 7-week stay. I packed my bags with all the 'essentials' to share with others on my trip, which included silly things such as peanut butter (which the missionary priests loved!) and *M'n'M's*. My friend and I

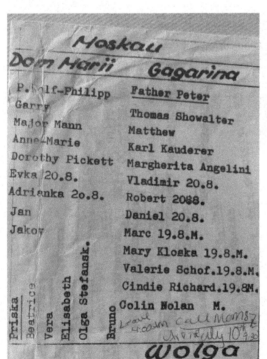

were planning to take a bus to Chicago together, and then fly to New York where we would meet up with a few other people volunteering for the summer. From there we flew to Austria and then took a bus to Slovakia where we were to have a one-week retreat to prepare us for our work in Russia. At the end of our one-week retreat we were each given a loaf of bread and a stick of salami as our ration of food for the train, and then climbed on another bus, which took us to the train station for our 1 ½ day train ride into Moscow.

This train ride itself was a powerful experience. As we traveled through the Ukraine, we had several Masses in the different little compartments all at one time, each in a different language. There must have been 15 or more of us crammed into the English Mass. After Mass, one of the priests brought Jesus in a pix into each of our compartments for a half-hour of Eucharistic Adoration. It was truly beautiful.

I remember that while we were going through the Ukraine, I saw out of a window a group of little kids from a nearby village playing on a hill near the tracks. A few of the little boys were picking on one of the younger ones, and they pushed him down. My heart felt helpless as we whizzed by the scene and I was unable to run to this little one and help or defend him. That helpless feeling of being unable to 'fix' all the problems and sufferings around me would only grow as I traveled deeper into the heart of

Russia. This was a land of wounded hearts, as a priest told us in his homily on the train. America often has cold hearts—people simply indifferent to God. But Russia is a land of wounded hearts. The people may seem cold or hard, but they are only wounded. If we loved them, he said, then they would

quickly break open before us and drink this love. And this truth I would see with my own eyes.

Moscow—Summer 1994

When we arrived in Moscow (there were probably 40 of us in all) it was late in the evening. I was so happy to be greeted at

Dom Marie[1] with a warm meal of some sort of chili, and cookies. Never had a meal tasted so good to be before!

---

[1] Dom Marie, meaning 'House of Mary' in Russian, was the name given to this central mission house in Moscow.

I remember that my first impression of Russia was the great darkness I felt in Moscow. It was a darkness of pure evil, which I had never before experienced to such a degree. The first night before I went to bed I was praying in the little chapel before Jesus in the Tabernacle. The American priest who was to head up our little mission was also praying in there, and I heard Jesus tell me to ask him for his blessing. My heart felt as if on fire with this urge, yet in my pride I felt 'stupid' and was too embarrassed to ask. And so, I went to bed, without obeying Jesus and without this priest's blessing. That night I was awakened all night with nightmares. I kicked and yelled so loudly that I woke up my friend, who had to share the top bunk with me because of our shortage of beds. I had seen in my dream the faces of lots of little demons flying around the ceiling of our room. And I felt their evil. I regretted greatly that

I had not asked the priest for his blessing the night before. The next morning as soon as I saw him, I recounted to him what had happened (both in the chapel and in my room that night) and he told me to please never fear to ask a priest for a blessing. He then promptly gave me his.

Many of the missionaries that came with us on the train were planning to head off to their various assigned missions for the summer —which stretched from the south of Moscow all the way to Eastern Siberia— the following day or two. My friend, another youth group friend (who last

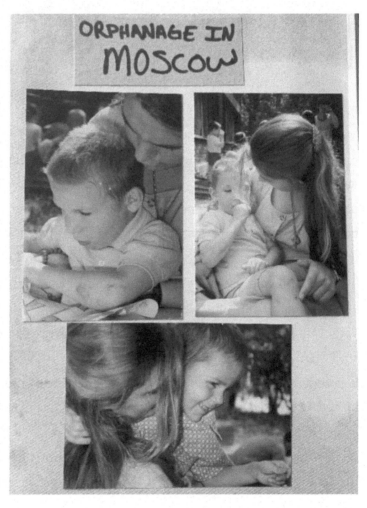

ORPHANAGE IN MOSCOW

minute was allowed to join us), and I were all assigned to a summer mission in a little village near Moscow, called Gagarinka. We would remain for a week in Moscow as the American SOLT priest and seminarian (the heads of our mission) were sent ahead of us to prepare.

Jesus had prepared many little blessings for me that week I spent in Moscow. That week (and entire summer as a matter of fact) was so short yet seemed like an eternity of time to me. In Dom Marie was also living a young girl with her newborn baby; she had been on drugs when she was pregnant, and so this little one was suffering. No one could seem to quiet the little girl at times, and so they allowed me to take her when she cried. I would hold her very secure and still and pray that Our Heavenly Mother would calm her little heart. And I do not remember a time when this did not work. I loved this time of babysitting Tatiana. She nestled her way deep into my heart.

Dom Marie had a soup kitchen through which they fed lunch to the poorest of people in the neighborhood. I remember also helping out in this work; they asked me to simply keep all of the people, most of whom were babushkas,[2] in an orderly line as they waited their turn to eat. This was very difficult for me, not only because they were not very cooperative, but also because the odor from them made me sick. Although I often cuddled 'smelly'

---

[2] Babushka is the Russian word for grandma and is used to describe any older lady.

children at CAPS,[3] I still had not learned to let the love of God and love for my neighbors overrule my sense of smell. When a fight broke out between two of the babushkas, I ran to get someone to help. I could not speak the language, and although they were older babushkas, they physically were quite strong.

I also was able to visit an orphanage a few times in this week I stayed in Moscow. This was a work I deeply loved, and yet which deeply saddened my heart. When we first arrived, we were led through the little building where the children lived and ate. It seemed filthy dirty to me, and the stench was awful. *"How can these children live here, in such a place?"* I wondered. We were led upstairs into one very clean, bright, neat little room. This is where all the caretakers gathered. These few women were all in this room smoking and watching TV. I was appalled. *"Where are the children and who is with them?"* I wondered. As we were led downstairs and outdoors by one of the sisters with us, I found my answer. The children were outside playing in the woods nearby, and no one was watching them. I would come to hear similar and much worse stories about such government-run orphanages throughout Russia in the two years I would spend serving in Siberia. Most of these children were found on the streets, abandoned by alcoholic parents. The most recent arrival, I was told, was a family of three:

---

[3] CAPS stands for Child Abuse Prevention Services—it was an organization that worked to help prevent child abuse as well as to heal children who had been abused. I had worked for 5 years caring for children while their parents attended various workshops and classes.

the 7-year-old sister had cared for her 5 and 2-year-old siblings for months on the streets. When the authorities asked them where their parents lived, they refused to answer fearing that they would be returned to them. The children were almost all unclothed, wearing only underwear or a ragged, hole-filled tee-shirt. I thought that they were all boys because of their shaved heads. Yet I would come to find out later that this was done for health purposes, and that half of them actually were girls. They were absolutely starved for love and attention.

As we approached the backyard area, I was forced to sit right down on the dirt ground as a handful of children (ages 2 ½ to about 8-years-old) ran to me, climbing on my lap and shoulders. I did not speak their language, but they did not care. They wanted only love. I spent the duration of our time there—and the time on our next visits—simply doing one thing: sitting, holding, and listening to these children whom I did not understand with my mind, yet wonderfully understood with my heart. I simply tried to let Jesus pour out all the love He could on them from within me. When I asked if these children would eventually be adopted, I received the sad answer of 'probably not'—their caretakers were greedy and wanted too much money for each child, one of the sisters told me. It was all so complicated—a tangled mess in Russia. *"But what could you expect?"* I thought, *"For this country was run by the devil himself for 80 years!"*

The neighborhood in Moscow where our mission Dom Marie was located looked to me like the 'Projects' of Chicago, although I was told that the surrounding neighborhood was by far not the worst in Moscow. "This is normal, middle-class," they told me. Yet that did not mean it was completely safe. We girls were told to not go outside alone—a seminarian had to be with us for protection. And one evening one of our priests pulled a prostitute who lived above us into Dom Marie, saving her from being stabbed to death by an angry man outside our door. The few evenings I sat outside together with some other mission-workers my heart felt very heavy from the world I saw around me. One evening, I will never forget, I watched a drunken woman stumbling home with a little child (no older than 2-years-old) flung over her shoulder like a sack of potatoes. He was wide-eyed and expressionless. *"From where was this woman coming and why was this child with her in such a place? If this child experienced these things in the daytime and early evening, what kind of horrors did he experience at night?"* I wondered. That image grafted itself into my heart, and I simply prayed for them. What more could I do? I simply prayed for them.

Although the hopelessness of Russia seemed to push heavy into my heart, I also did have a few good experiences with the ladies of our neighborhood. One day as I took a walk down to the nearby park (about 50m from our home), I passed by a group of gossiping older women. They all stopped talking as I passed them by, watching me. And I simply smiled. On my walk back, as they did the same as before—simply watching me together in silence—I walked up to one of them and gave them a miraculous medal saying, "Mater Bosha" as I had learned (Russian for "Mother of God"). I turned to walk away and after a few steps I heard yelling after me. One woman came up, falling on her knees before me in thanksgiving, kissing my hands, and through her tears she began saying many names and counting on her fingers. I figured that she just wanted more medals for her family, and as I handed her a handful, she kissed my hands once more crying, "Spaceeba, Spaceeba," meaning, "Thank you, thank you." I was in some ways amazed at her response to such a little gesture of mine. But as I pondered this incident, it all began to make sense to me. For so many years people all over the world had prayed for 'the conversion of Russia' as Our Lady had asked in Fatima. And all these prayers filled the vacuum air of Russia with the 'gasoline' of many graces. All that was needed was a little act of love, a spark (like my act of giving a simple medal), to set their hearts on fire.

The Village of Gagarinka—Summer 1994

After our work in Moscow, Val (the other young girl from America) and I were sent to spend the rest of our summer in a little, nearby village called Gagarinka. This village was very little, consisting of maybe 40 homes and two hospital-like institutions all centered on a destroyed Orthodox Church.

The house where we lived was still being constructed, yet that did not bother us from making ourselves at home. This house was to be a rehabilitation center for drug addicts from Moscow. It had no toilet except for the outhouse out back and no running water.

Our water had to be carried in big metal buckets from a spring about a half-mile away. My heart fell in love with this place and the life we led there. It was so simple. It reminded me of how Our Lady must have lived—of how God intended for us to live. We worked, prayed, and played (games of baseball from logs and rocks we found out back). And that was it. Various people came through that house that summer; I had counted at its maximum 30 people living there. This included missionaries, those who ran the program for drug addicts, and the ex-drug addicts themselves. One meal I remember counting seven different languages being spoken at once. My favorite place in the entire house was our third-floor chapel. There I spent many hours in prayer.

There were two little boys, 2 and 3-years-old, who also lived with us for a short time in Gagarinka. Their mom was somehow connected with the rehabilitation program, and their dad was in Moscow—an abusive alcoholic. When I first arrived, I was so excited about these children; the seminarians there warned me not to be excited because these kids were 'monsters,' they said. Yet I disregarded their warnings. I had worked at a child abuse prevention center with very abused and difficult children, and I had never met with a child that a lot of love could not reach. As I bent down to say 'hi' to little Nikita, who was hiding behind a chair, he looked at me and punched me right in my face. And I quickly learned that these kids truly needed 'special love'. They were horribly misbehaved—no one wanted to watch them, and no one could control them. At the end of their stay, these children would play with me a bit; and the younger one even let me hold him. This gave me joy that they finally let me love them; yet I still knew what kind of future they had, and I was saddened. Yet I did all I knew to –I prayed for them a lot and left them in the hands of God.

The first question I was asked when we arrived at our village mission home was if one of us by any chance had any sort of eye medication. Serge, one of the ex-drug addicts, had somehow gotten a deep infection in his eye. Father had told him that if God did not send medicine that day, he would have to go to the hospital. Well, to their surprise, I had an eye antibiotic that my mom had gotten for me 'just in case' I was to need it. They rejoiced at God's great providence through the thoughtful heart of my mother. I began giving Serge eye drops a few times a day.

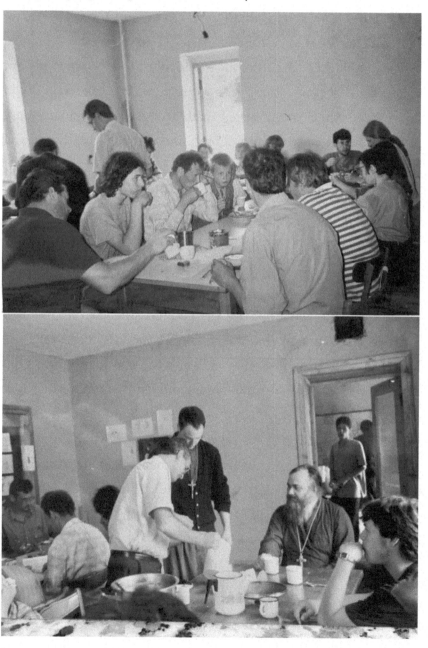

I was scandalized by the great poverty the Russians were forced to live. We received donations of food—left over army rations from Germany, huge cans of ravioli from Italy, and very greasy canned beef from somewhere else. Yet sometimes we had to go to the store (for our mission family was large and ate a lot), and this was an unforgettable experience for me. The shelves of these stores seemed to be almost empty, except for maybe a piece of clothing, a bucket, an icon, and a loaf of bread. And trying to create a meal from such a mishmash of food was so difficult.

My work in Gagarinka that summer varied day

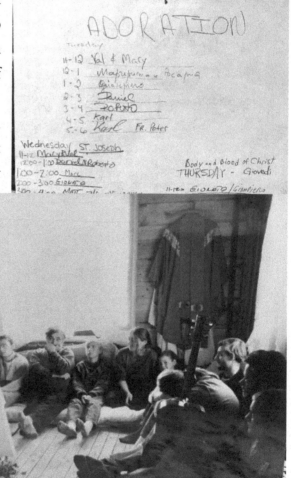

to day. As most of the men's time at the beginning was being spent on physically building the house, I was assigned at first to kitchen duty.

This, above all, meant organization of all the boxes of donated goods covering the floors. I spent hours with my friend, cleaning and sorting, only for the next day all to be ruined as they repaired something in the kitchen, dirtying the room again, or received more boxes of new donations and moved all I had organized.

A few days in a row we spent re-cleaning and re-sorting, until finally we gave up, leaving that work for another to accomplish after construction had ended. We each took turns preparing meals and we had a 'dish washing schedule' from which we rotated doing dishes in the morning and at night. I remember on one occasion Father asked Val and me to do the laundry for all the men working (along with our own). This consisted of lugging big basins of water

from the spring a half-mile away, and cleaning everything by hand. And after the clothes were clean, we had to sit by them as they dried in the sun, watching them so that some of the villagers would not come steal them.

Often, I would go to Father in the morning and ask him what I could do that day, and he would answer by tell-ing me to go into the chapel and pray for them all day. I loved these hours I spent

alone with Jesus in love. It was in that little chapel where I first learned the key to mission life in Russia. Prayer with Jesus in the Blessed Sacrament would have to be the foundation and center of all we did not only in that mission

in Gagarinka that summer, but in any mission, I would help with in the future as well. Only the powerful Love flowing from Jesus' Eucharistic Heart could change, heal, and help the wounded hearts we would encounter. My favorite time of day was at night when we would rotate turns in Adoration.

Adoration would begin at 10:00pm and continue until our Mass at 8:00am. When our house was full, one or two of us would

'sign up' for an hour with Jesus. Later in the summer when the drug addicts left for a retreat pilgrimage to Medjugorje, we were left with many fewer people to pray at night. The suggestion was made that we shorten the Adoration time since we had too few people. Yet I in my boldness threw a fit, offering to take 3 or 4 hours at night if need be, just so that this time of Adoration could remain. And my dear, patient priest agreed. I believed that the most important work that we did as missionaries was encompassed in those long hours praying before our Lord at night. To love Him among the Russians was our first and primary work, for He was the Source of all. There was so much I saw around me that I could not do to help these people. Yet I believed that if we sat before Jesus and allowed Him to pour graces through our hearts into the Russian land surrounding us, then His Love could do miracles there. Our call, I felt, was to simply sit as portals of His grace and Love, to provide a resting place for the Holy Spirit and His Love. Before we could change

the lives of people, we had to first simply love God among them so that they, too, could come to know Him and love Him. Many graces were 'snuck' into Russia in those long nights of prayer. We were the only place for hundreds of miles where Jesus was being adored all night.

I also spent some time during the day helping to clean out the ruined nearby Orthodox church. It had been taken over by the Communists after the Revolution and had been turned into a sawmill and then a movie theater before it was left abandoned and claimed by the gypsies as a place to live. Its floor had been destroyed as well as all its structures within, except for the faint frescos still visible high up on the walls. More than anything, the

greatest symbol to me was the Holy Spirit whose wings brightly spread over the ceiling of the highest dome. They destroyed this church, but they could not destroy Him. Our mission in Gagarinka had a good relationship with the local Orthodox priest and we were trying to clean the church up a bit for him, so that he could begin construction of a new one.

The most difficult work that I did that summer was in visiting the boys and men at the 'hospital' institution in the center of the village. This place truly showed me what the ugly face of Communism did to human dignity. Often in Russia, people considered 'out casts' in society—the elderly, handicapped or even

sometimes simply children of divorce I was told—were sent 'away' to institutions in the country. This 'hospital' was in-humane, as the men and boys were kept in cages (locked wooden sheds with barbed wire on the openings, although the barbed wire had been temporarily taken down the summer when I was visiting). The 'nurses' would leave these boys and men locked up like this all day, to beat each other and go to the bathroom on themselves. The 'nurses' often beat these poor

victims, which caused all those who were mentally normal when they first came to quickly become mentally handicapped as well. These were truly the victim souls of Russia, suffering with a Jesus they did not know. Little Dema was their angel. He was 18 and sick with some sort of mental handicap (as well as some physical handicap, for he was only half my height). He was always smiling and helping his brothers. He was the one who on occasion would bathe them; and he was the one who snuck us into the house to pray with his dying friend. He did not speak but smiled in the midst of the nightmare he lived. He was these men's hope—for he loved them for Jesus, a Jesus he did not know. He was holy.

I would go down to visit my suffering brothers often during the week, trying to bring them as much love as I could muster. I would often sing to them "Jesus Love Me," and simply hold their hands. Sometimes, we would let them out of their cages to play with them the simple games of ball or drawing with chalk that we brought with us. When the nurses would come running, yelling at us for unlocking the doors, we would smile and say, "Ya nee ponnee-mayou," which meant, "I don't understand." It took much of Jesus' grace and merciful Love to get me to spend the long hours that I did with these men. My

heart was very broken for them, and I wanted desperately to love them, but I felt like I did not know how, and my body was disgusted by their smell of urine and bloody sores. Yet somehow Jesus mustered up courage for me, and day after day I would go to visit them.

One day our priest decided that we would all go down to bathe them. We had received donations of clean clothes for them, yet we had been warned about simply giving these to the caretakers because often they (in their 'need') would steal them, taking them

home. Even if we were to clothe the men ourselves, it was better for us to take their old clothes with us to burn; other-wise, the nurses would change them back into their old, ripped, filthy clothes so that they could take the better ones home. And so this is what we planned to do. We would go down to the hospital to bathe the men, change their clothes and take their old ones home with us to burn. The morning that we planned to go, I went to Confession to Father. At the end, he asked me if I was ready to go with them to the hospital, and I replied, "Oh, Father, I am not going with you."

"What?" he asked.

I said, "I just can't! Do you know how I hate going down there?! It is so hard for me. It is just so sad. No, I just can't make myself go."

And he said to me, "Mary, you have a very special gift. A gift we have all noticed—it is the gift of Love. We have all been watching you, and we agree that out of all of us, you are the best one with those men, for you truly love

Village People

ANNA, SASHA, JENA

them. And when God gives a gift like yours, He gives it with a responsibility that we use it. You **must** go with us today. It is your responsibility because God gave you the gift of Love."

And then he got up and left the chapel saying, "See you there." I was stuck. I had to go. I heard them all leave, and my heart pulled me to go with them. So, I said a prayer and trudged downstairs and out on to the little, dirt road praying, "Oh, Jesus, help me!"

When I arrived at the hospital, Father gave me what sounded to be a simple job: to keep the men in a line. Well, this was a huge challenge, as they so rarely got a bath and were so excited to receive one that they began stripping themselves naked right there and fighting over who was next. I had to laugh as I tried to keep them dressed (for my modesty's sake) and not beating each other up. In

the end, our 'Operation Bath' worked, and all were clean and happy. *"Their bodies were clean, but how wounded were their hearts?"* I pondered. *"How could people suffer so deeply without Jesus and still live?"* It was a sad, dark question for me. I gathered these men all up in my heart, along with the orphans, baby Tatiana and all those I encountered in Russia, and I prayed ardently for them, day after day, long after I returned home. These people are some of the treasures in my heart that I can give Jesus today as He lifts me to be one with Him on Calvary. As His crucified Love consumes me, may it also consume them, giving meaning, hope, and life to all the horror they endured.

Many things happened that shocked me that summer. One day as I was returning from my work at the hospital, an old babushka came running up to me crying hysterically. I feared that something tragic had happened, as I thought she was pointing towards the direction of the hospital. *"Maybe one of the men was beaten to death,"* I thought. I just did not know, and I could not understand a word of Russian although she was trying to explain something to me between her sobs. Suddenly she began to collapse on me, and I was not strong enough to hold her up. Looking down the road, clueless as to what to do, I saw Father and one of the seminarians walking my way. I called to them and yelled, "Run!" As they began to run to me, this old woman fell through my arms onto the ground, as she was too big for me to hold up. When my help arrived I tried to explain as much of this confusion as I could, and when they picked up her purse all became clear. Vodka poured out from its bottom in a stream. She must have just been drunk and passed out. Father and the seminarian tried to pick her up, which was very difficult as she was a large woman. In the end, they simply took her arms and legs and carried her towards the village where we met a woman (who must have been her daughter) standing by the door of her house motioning for them to bring her there. As we entered the house, they laid the babushka down somewhere to rest, and we were offered tea and cookies (as is the Russian hospitable thing to do for guests.) The lady of the house proceeded to show us all of her old icons and holy things that she had hidden and treasured during the long years of Communism. She must have been a believer. It was so sad to me how lost these people were; their lives were so dark that they would drink themselves to death just to forget. Oh, Jesus on Calvary, I thank You for the gift of Your Mother to us. I especially thank You for giving Her to the poor people of Russia, for She is their Mother in a special way. She is their Mother of hope. Please, save these people, heal these people so deeply wounded, through Her prayerful intercession. And may Your Love in Her heart truly triumph in such darkness—triumph in Russia and throughout the whole world.

On August 16th, my friend and I were heading back to Moscow for a few days and then on to America as my senior year of high school was about to begin. August 15th was the Feast of the Assumption, and our priest decided that we would make it a big village feast that year. We planned to begin with Mass in the old, abandoned Orthodox church and then to take the Blessed Sacrament in a procession to bless each house in the village. We would conclude with a big village meal for everyone at our house. We spent all night without sleep cleaning and cooking. The morning of August 15th Father gave my friend and me the job of going to the hospital to bring the men to our Mass in the church. Someone had already spoken to one of the nurses and received permission. We went down and began leading a few to the church, situating them within, and then returning to bring more. Yet after we had only moved a handful of men, the head-nurse returned from out of town; and when she knew of what we were doing she wanted to stop it. She said that we could keep the men we had but take no more. So, I said to the others helping, "Run!" and we each picked up one more person and carried them to the church. These men and boys had so greatly suffered, I really wanted them to be at Mass just once in their lives so that they could meet face to Face with Jesus—for Whom and with Whom they suffered. The Mass, procession and meal all went beautifully. A few of us helped the handicapped even walk in the procession with Jesus. And when they were fed, we sadly took them back to the hospital. After we cleaned up, we had to quickly prepare our bags, for we would leave the next morning for Moscow and then for home. I remember being exhausted.

I see now how immature I was in my mission work that first trip to Russia, how often I spent that summer on myself in little ways, seeking my comfort and not giving myself fully. I regretted this after I returned home, feeling like I had not focused on God enough and had not always done His will. I believe it was His great mercy to me that He allowed for me to return to serve in Russia many years later with a more deeply spiritual and mature heart. I believe that that summer when I was 17, I tried to give Russia my heart, and I failed with my many weaknesses, wounds, sins, and imperfections. Yet when I was to return years later, I would try to give Russia Jesus' Heart, Who slowly had begun to live in me in the place of my own. As I had begun to see my great weaknesses and failures and had offered them to Jesus' Light, He was able to clear me of them making a place where He and His Love could enter, rule, live, and love from within me. And His Love and Heart was the best medicine I could give to these wounded people whom I had grown to love.

I believe that in the summer of 1994 I met Russia—I first saw her face, her emotions, and her thoughts. And I pitied her. But I did not know her heart. It would only be years later, when I returned to serve in Siberia (located physically in the 'heart' of Russia), that Jesus would begin to help me know and love the spiritual heart of the Russians. And this Russian heart was the place Jesus would place His Love—deep within her to heal her and make her new—and that, in turn, would transform her face, emotions, and thoughts to reflect His Light in the world.

That summer opened in me a deep love for Russia and a thirst to serve her in the missions; it was a thirst Jesus would stretch and prune for years before He would lead me back to serve there again. Yet more than anything, I fell in love with Jesus that summer in a new way. I had never really loved Him as a person, intimately as my Beloved, until He showed me His Face that summer. He showed me His Face in Russia's poverty, in contrast with her darkness, in my suffering brothers and sisters, in the powerful homilies that Father gave, and especially in the long hours I spent with Him in Adoration at night. This love for Jesus, which grew within me in the midst of a Russia that did not know Him, was the greatest gift I received that summer. God would lead me again to Russia to reveal my vocation to me and to unite deeply with me, healing me in His school of suffering Love. I loved Russia not for Russia, but for the Jesus I fell in love with there. Yet my heart was not made 'Russian' by this experience; instead, my heart was made 'His'. And Jesus would use Russia to teach me of His suffering Heart, so that He could take me even from this mission so I could go deeper in His Love, living one with His Heart on the Cross. In some ways, I will always love Russia, but it is only because of my Sweet Jesus Who so deeply revealed His Heart to me there (and Who also so deeply loves her). If I received so many graces in my life from my time of serving in the missions there, I have no doubt that Jesus truly is with these people, especially in their suffering and blindness to Him. And I do not have a doubt that someday Russia will be converted and be a great Light of contradiction, a Light of Jesus' Love in the world. And so, I lay the Russia I love in Jesus' hands as well, to heal, hold and love. Amen. Alleluia.

Chapter 3

The Russian Heart

During the school year following my first mission trip to Russia, I had a powerful dream in which Our Lady came alive out of a statue and spoke to me saying, "*Just as my children need you here, they need you in Russia. Go to them.*" This set afire in my heart a strong desire to return to Russia once more. And I had another opportunity to do so that following summer, but my mother's great worry prevented me from going. Although my father had given me permission, I resigned myself to remain in America (out of love for my mother) and to instead offer up the great suffering in my heart (a suffering of desire and love) for all those I could not physically serve in the mission that summer. My great love for the mission in Russia continued to follow me for many years after I returned home the summer of 1994. I eventually went on to study at the University of Notre Dame and decided to major in Russian, hoping I could use that by giving my life to the missions there someday. Eventually, I changed my major, but my love for Russia continued to grow. After I finished school, I went to spend some time in prayer, living with some hermits. During this period, an increasing fire to return to Russia quietly began to rage in the bottom of my heart again. And so, as a fly-by-night chance in the summer of 2000, I found an old phone number of the religious community of the priest and seminarian with whom I had worked in Russia when I was seventeen. I had heard that the seminarian, who was by then a priest, was planning to go back to Russia to start his own mission with his community. And so desperate to find God's will for my life I decided to try to follow this growing desire in my heart—I decided to 'wing it' and call this number to see if I could go back to Russia to their mission somehow.

And so, through God's divine intervention, I was invited in the end to join one SOLT sister who would be traveling to Siberia to set up a new mission that following summer. (The priest I had contacted had been prevented from returning himself because of heart problems.) Several months before I left for Russia in June 2001, I fell asleep in Adoration one night and had a very prophetic dream about the upcoming mission. This dream accurately portrayed the great evil that I was about to encounter in Russia and the mission Jesus laid out for me there—which was to love and treasure His abused Eucharistic Heart. The dream was as follows:

I fell asleep at Adoration and I had a really disturbing dream—I don't know why since I was at Adoration, but maybe it had a meaning. Here it is:

I was at Adoration (in my dream) and when I left the chapel I immediately saw outside as I was walking this 'house', although it looked like a stand for food…(like a Russian kiosk)…Inside of it were two scary, dirty, horrifying men and a little baby boy (I could tell he was a boy because he was basically naked— all he had on was a ripped T-shirt). The baby was probably 1½-years-old. His hair was long. He was so dirty. The men were hurting him, laughing and He was crying. His body was covered in bugs. He had welts all over Him and many places on His body that were raw blisters oozing water and blood. On His arms and hands He had cigarette burns almost 1 inch deep. Some of these wounds were fresh, some were old. I did not know that anyone could be so abused. In some places His flesh was almost hanging off of Him.[4] *I went up to the men who were mocking and roughing Him. They were roughly trying to put a plastic bag around Him almost like a diaper. (The way they were doing this reminded me of sexual abuse). I asked if I could have Him for a while and they said that if He would go to me, I could take Him. I was with my friend from S.O.L.T. and at first He stared crying and maybe reaching for her, but when I picked Him up He clung to me and immediately I was alone with Him on the street. I took Him back to the place with the chapel where I had been praying. The location of the dream was very clear and foreign. I knew that the men did not know why they had allowed me to take the child. As soon as I had taken Him, they became mad and wanted to search for Him. As I was trying to protect Him, I noticed from behind me the 'house' from which I had taken the child. The mean men were there, as well as twenty-some other men, looking clean cut and a little effeminate. They went into the woods and changed into these priest's clothes. They were not wearing the clothes neatly or respectfully and they scared me. I went home and tried to find someone to help me care for the Child, but I could trust no one. All the while I carried Him, I tried so hard to love Him and comfort Him even though, I'm embarrassed to say, His physical state repulsed my natural*

---

[4] When I saw the movie *The Passion* and how Jesus was ripped up by the scourging I thought of this dream and how the little boy in it looked just like Jesus—their wounds were similar in how bad, deep and horrifying they were to look at.

sentiments. Eventually I found my friend again and I wanted to bathe this little boy and then to call CAPS or some agency to help me save Him, but I could not. I also knew that I would be 'in trouble' for doing what I had in taking Him, but I kept reminding myself (and gaining courage in the thought) that this Child was a person and had to be saved even if I had to sacrifice my life for it. I felt like those men wanted to kill me. My friend was driving us in the car, looking for somewhere we could go for help, but we were in a weird, dangerous spot and I feared someone would take this Child from me. We drove by the 'house' from which I had taken the Child and I was so afraid that they would take Him that I ducked and begged her to not take us there but she drove around it anyway—I feared losing Him so much. By the house this time were those 'priests' together with all the police from the city who were also corrupt and would not have helped, but instead hurt the Child. So I kept Him close to my heart. I was confused as to whether the priests were going to do bad things dressed up as priests only to scandalize the Church (like they used the clothes of priests to purposely do bad things to the Church) or if they were infiltrating the Church to 'fake' things. I knew they were evil and out to destroy one way or the other. I finally in the end took the Child back with me into the chapel where I was in adoration and then I woke up. When I awoke, I was not filled with anything but peace in my heart, although my mind was confused by the dream (and my heart hurt for that Child.) I wondered if it was prophetic, and I felt like the Child was baby Jesus.

This dream profoundly affected me and etched itself in every detail in my mind, so that I can still see it all clearly up to the present day. The exact meaning is a mystery, but there are many symbols I did later recognize in it. The Child was little Jesus who was so abused (both in His own Eucharistic Body as well as in the body of His little children and all the people of the Church in Russia). And it was true in Russia when I found children hurting and abandoned that I felt I could not trust anybody with them. Often those who should have helped these children would take advantage of them and abuse them. The Orthodox Church in Russia had been infiltrated during Communism by all sorts of evil and political people. And the police were just as corrupt as the Church. Often people were harmed because they wanted to help others, especially if they tried to love or protect Jesus and His Church. And my personal vocation not only in Russia, but also in all my life, is to hold Jesus' wounded little Heart and allow it to rest in mine. It is to care for and love His wounds. It is to let His wounds be so important to me that I sacrifice my whole life for them.

I loved Russia because in it I found my Jesus Crucified. I know that I was attracted to Russia not because of the culture or the language (which was beautiful), but because there I found the poorest, most suffering people I had ever heard of or met in the whole world—and they suffered so much with Jesus, but with a

Jesus they did not know. One night during the weeks leading up to my departure for Siberia I read an article written in a newspaper by Catherine Doherty, a Russian born immigrant to Canada who founded a spiritual community under her Archbishop there. She was writing about a childhood memory she had, when an old woman pilgrim[5] came to her house to spend the night. This old woman told a fascinating story about a meeting with the devil, a prophecy of the ruin of the Russian people (this was before Communism came), a meeting with Our Lady and a message of hope. The devil appeared to this old lady in the form of a man, and he began to fill the old woman's thoughts with great doubt about her Catholic faith. When the man began to outright mock the Blessed Virgin and those people who believe in her virginity, she realized that he was pure evil. The woman was afraid and so took some holy water in her pocket and threw it on the man. He shrieked, fell to the ground, and disappeared. But before he did so he said, *"You old fool! All Russia will be covered with rivers of blood over the things I've said. Millions will think like I do. There will be moaning and groaning and tears all over this land. I am out to win it, and win it I will. And neither your God nor*

---

[5] I use the word pilgrim in the Russian sense of the word. Before communism, Russians often went on 'pilgrimages' on foot to religious shrines once a year. It did not matter how far it was; they walked. They carried only a little water, bread, and salt. They wore special clothes and a little icon around their necks. They stopped at villages in the evenings to stay with random people for the night. It was considered an honor to welcome a pilgrim into your home.

your Blessed Virgin will be able to save it." This experience and these words so terrified this old woman that she fainted, yet when she woke up, she met another woman, dressed in a very simple pilgrim's clothing and who was very beautiful. It was our heavenly Mother. The words of Our Mother to this poor, scared, little pilgrim lady set my heart on fire. She said, *"Fear not, Grandma, it is true what the man said, but he was not a man. These things will come to pass so that holy Russia may hang on the Cross with my Son to redeem the world. The only way the world can be redeemed is through suffering with my Son. Fear not. There will come a day, when, under the sign of my Son, I will lead Russia to show my Son's face to the world..."* These words brought tears to my eyes. I fell in love with Mary's words **"Russia will be hung on the Cross...to show my Son's Crucified Face to the world."** That is why I fell in love with Russia, I believe. Because from the first moments I had ever heard of that country when I was little (and I was told how people suffered there and that we needed to pray for Russia's conversion), I saw my Jesus' sad, suffering face in them.

As I wrote before, although I had seen Russia in my first trip when I was 17 years old, I did not come to deeply know the Russian heart until I had spent a couple of years in Siberia. In many ways, sister and I were clueless those first months, and we were similar to two blind people trying to feel their way around an unfamiliar room without falling. Yet, in reflecting on those first months with the light of the Holy Spirit, I see that God's grace profoundly guided us way before we understood with our minds these people we lived among and served. I am amazed that God somehow created a beautiful dance between these unfamiliar people, His grace, and the different wounds and gifts of our own hearts.

There is something very deep about the Russian heart. Such depth and strength enabled millions of Catholics and Orthodox to remain faithful to their beliefs when Communism took over their country and to willingly suffer martyrdom for them. This strength of faith led the people of one village outside of Moscow to gather around the grave of their martyred priest (shortly after Communism began) so that they could confess their sins to him (even if he was dead) when they were left shepherdless. And yet the Russian heart has also been very wounded by the evil of Communism scourging it from every side for 80 years. It is a heart that today (like so many other countries' hearts) is often drowning in sin. It is a heart that is closed by fear. Yet it is a heart that is very profound and thoughtful—it is a heart that feels deeply and thinks deeply. Russia has a very mysterious heart which somehow communes with God even if from behind the veil of darkness that has overshadowed her. I know this because I have met His presence in many different forms among the people I have served there. He has reached out and taught me through them, and because of this I always will say that in the few years that I have served in Russia, Russia gave me way more than I could ever have given her. She was an instrument through which God's grace poured into my heart. She was a living icon of my Beloved Jesus' crucified Heart suffering darkness on the Cross.

When a missionary goes to serve among a people his or her job is not to 'bring them God.' Instead, the work of a missionary is to find where God is already living and present among a people and to show Him to them. It is to help people discover His Love beating from His Heart already living among them. One day, when I walked into a building in St. Petersburg to visit some friends' monastery located in an apartment there, I was overtaken by the beauty of the architecture, and I exclaimed to the priest and seminarian with me, "What a beautiful building!" They, of course, looked at me as if I was a bit crazy, for the staircase we were walking through was dirty with paint and wood chipping off of the walls and railing. I responded to their looks with this answer, "This building is very beautiful. It just needs to be cleaned up and repaired a little. But there is beauty here…" I continued to think of how similar this situation was to any missionary's life, for when a missionary goes into a poor or spiritually dark place in order to serve, *God is there*. When a missionary finds a heart deep in sin or lost in sorrow, he immediately must remember that *God is there*, somewhere underneath the mess or dirt or brokenness. And the work of a missionary is to find the beauty, the truth, the Love of God's presence already in that situation, in that person's heart, and to show it to them. And this is why the source of every missionary's work must be Jesus' great act of Love for us on the Cross. On the Cross, Jesus entered the greatest darkness and took all of humanity's sin upon Himself and filled these horrible things with His Saving Love. When a person meets the face of the Man of

Sorrows on Calvary's path there does not seem to be anything pretty about it, yet Jesus' Way of the Cross and Crucificial Gift of Himself in death had a very deep, profound hidden beauty within it—it was the beauty of His Love. His answer to the darkness, the sin, the death was an answer of Love, surrender, obedience, and trust and that was very, very beautiful.

When I first traveled to Russia, I quickly came to see how there were so many great problems in the hearts and lives of these people—abortions, sexual abuse, alcoholism, physical destitution, hunger, anger, violence, fear, adultery and prostitution, pornography, and so much more. The people of Russia were being crucified by suffering and darkness, but through Communism Jesus had been seemingly stolen from their cross. And the cross, the crucifixion, without God is hell—for it is senseless suffering. I quickly realized that I could not go into Russia and fix all of her many problems. No, I could not put 'band-aids' on all of her wounds, for new wounds were continually appearing on her body from her sickness of heart deep within. I realized that the first and greatest work to be done in Russia—the only real way to help heal her deeply—was to go to her cross, climb on it and suffer on it with her; to show her where God, where Jesus is on that cross with her; to carry His presence deep within my heart to them as a witness that He does exist, especially in the deepest sufferings of their hearts and lives. Only in this, in showing Jesus' suffering Heart full of Love and mercy to them in the midst of their problems, could their hearts be healed. And once their wounded hearts are healed, the rest of their societal problems would also begin to be resolved. I could not take all of their crosses from them, but I could teach them Jesus' answer of Love to these crosses—and in this answer of Love was all that they needed. When people in Russia asked me why I came there, I never answered 'to bring you God' or 'to teach you about God'. I always answered instead, "I simply came to Russia to love God among you" and "to love you for God." And only in this, loving His Crucified Heart, suffering in and among them, could their hearts begin to see, to thirst for, and to receive His great, healing, salvific Love for them.

Brokenness, Blessings, and The Great Paradox of Russia

Russia reminds me of one big, dysfunctional, classically alcoholic family. And when I look at her like that, I can find the patience I need to truly love her. The Russians say that "Russians themselves don't understand Russia," or "You cannot ever understand Russia, you simply must love her." When things break, fall apart, or end up in disordered, confused mayhem, Russians say as an excuse, "Well, that is Russia." They never seem to think that maybe there could be a way to fix a problem; instead, they very passively put up with it. They all remind me of a typically abused person who simply gets used to the abuse, or is led by fear, and therefore never tries to get out of the bad situation. In some ways, they have the virtue of patience, yet in other ways I think they are just wounded, immature, or underdeveloped. The great breakdown in Russia—from a lack of work ethic, to lack of order in government policies, to lack of morality, to lack of working toilets—is the effect of 80 years of Communist dictatorship over a people who are naturally simple and good followers. America is made up of immigrants who were strong willed, courageous leaders who left their own countries seeking to work hard and make a better life for themselves. America naturally has leaders and no patience for injustice. Yet Russia was run for many years by czars before Communism, and so the people are used to following 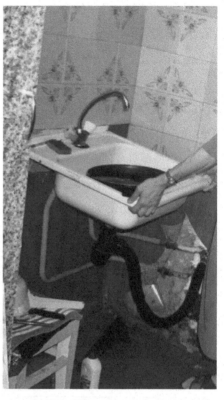 what they are told and simply accepting life as it is. Especially during Communism, everything was provided for them—food, apartment, education, job, clothes, and travel. I remember a man telling me that during Communism it cost him $10-15 to fly from Siberia to Moscow. Everything was cheap. Yet that seemingly secure lifestyle cost the people formation in morality and their own freedom. They had bread, but no God. They had a home given to them, but at any point they could disappear from that home for no apparent reason—either murdered or sent away to prison camps for being an 'offender against the people' without a clear explanation of their 'crime' ever given. And they were paid every week whether they worked or simply stood at the entrance to the factory smoking all day. The dignity of the human person was thrown away through communist ideology and replaced by a philosophy of 'a person is worth his work.' Productivity was their god. And so, people without God and without self-respect began to imitate their corrupt government in a life of cheating, laziness, and lying in order to 'be productive' and get what they wanted. Oh, it was so sad.

And now, after Communism supposedly was replaced by democracy in Russia (although a taxi driver in Moscow once joked to me that the only thing democratic about Russia now was that the mafia *voted* among themselves who would be elected), people are left without any sort of food, housing, clothes, work, as well as morality or a good work ethic. It is very difficult to be honest in Russia. Sister and I saw that immediately upon our arrival in Siberia in 2001. You *have* to pay people off (with money, or a box of chocolates) to get normal things done (like a package properly mailed to the US). You *have* to lie about your income (if

you have a job), or the unjust taxes would take 80-90% of your profits and your family would starve. That is just how things are run there. And nothing seems to work properly because people are pretty irresponsible. The governmental offices do not agree with each other for the proper process to get a visa, or mail a letter, or register your apartment. And everything breaks all the time—a real teacher of patience. Sister and I learned about the latter as soon as we moved into our little apartment. The hot and/or cold water was often turned off for no apparent reason—sometimes for a day or two, other times for a few weeks. When we had water, it was so yellow and dirty that it made my skin break out. A Russian priest told me that it was because something was wrong with the sewage and somehow it made the water bad, yet no one in this city of a million people seemed to care. "That is just Russia," they would say. The telephone also often broke—we were told that the telepho

ne lines in our part of the city were just old, and that they

sometimes crossed or did not work completely. And so big sections of the city would quietly suffer without working phone lines, instead of complaining or someone trying to come up with a plan to fix them.

The problems we met with were not only 'general' problems like these, yet also specific problems in our apartment and with the attitude of repairmen and our landlady. For example, there was a huge hole in the wall in our kitchen, and water was leaking down from a pipe there into the neighbor's apartment. When we asked our landlady about it (as the neighbors were rightfully frustrated), she told us that the solution was easy, and she took scotch tape and pulled the wallpaper over the hole and closed it up. That was seriously her solution—not to fix the pipe, not to fill in the hole, but rather just to scotch tape it closed. And this was a well-educated woman. We had problems with our toilet from the first day—it would not flush and sometimes it leaked. In the 1-½ years Sister and I lived in that apartment, we must have had 12 repairmen over to fix it, and it never worked. They did all sorts of funny things in the little bathroom and charged us a pretty penny for their work, yet the toilet down to the last day did not work right. We never could put toilet paper or anything down it, and often we had to bring buckets of water in to 'flush' it. And only a few of our electrical plugs worked. I remember finding humor in it all as I wrote a letter home to my family saying, *"I'm happy to announce I am writing this from the floor of my 'make-do' living room. (I am writing it on the floor because the only plug that works is on one side of the room and the only phone connector is on the*

other- even the computer gets to live stretched on the cross in Russia-
praise God!!"[6]

The funniest story about my initiation into normal, everyday, dysfunctional Russian life happened on the day that Sister and I planned to have the priests and other missionaries over for our 'apartment blessing' and a little dinner afterwards. I wrote home about the incident describing the humor, even in the midst of great tragedy:

And for the end of this letter I have a story, so unbelievable it is almost funny. When I think of it, I can't believe the following day really happened: Sister and I moved into our apartment two weeks ago on Friday. On the following Monday we had the Claretian priests, some sisters and some lay missionaries over for a house blessing (and I WAS going to make Italian dinner.) I say WAS. My day began when on the way to the Claretians for adoration I found an almost dead body. The man had been drunk, fell (or was hit) to the ground and his face was smashed in. I ran to the Claretians and they called an ambulance. Please pray for the men like this. The Claretians said it wasn't abnormal to find people like this on the streets. After I prayed, I returned home to make dinner to find we had no hot water. I made my zucchini bread dough. I began to cut things up to make tomato sauce and as I was ready to throw stuff on the stove and into the oven, I realized that

---

[6] September 21, 2001.

neither our stove nor our oven worked. And we had 15 people coming to dinner! I started getting creative. Sis ran to the corner store and then we cut a bunch of stuff up for a cold meal. After that I began my journey to the Claretians (who had a working oven) down the busy streets of Krasnoyarsk (imagine walking down the streets of Chicago) carrying a big pan of uncooked zucchini bread dough wrapped in a garbage bag (we didn't have a cover) when it started to rain. I was actually glad it was raining, because our shower didn't work and we didn't have hot water to even take a duck bath. After cooking the bread at the Claretians I carried it home and realized our toilet was broke (it still doesn't work). The blessing ended up being great anyway and we did enjoy ourselves. I will add I wasn't surprised a week later when our kitchen sink literally fell off the wall onto me as I was trying to do the dishes. People in Russia have poor work ethic, so we still need prayers that someone will fix our toilet, sink (held up now by a balancing act on a chair) and our molded wall falling apart in the kitchen. I thought you might find as much humor in this as I did. It is so beautiful that God allows us to live the splinters of the cross with the Russian people. Things just work very different here. Even Russians don't understand Russia. They say about themselves: don't try to understand Russia, simply love her. And I do. Sister and I are full of joy to be allowed the honor to live and work and pray here. God gives us many graces through the hardships—so many graces that we actually love the hardships.[7]

The disturbing incident I wrote at the beginning of this letter home about finding the dead body was another form of Russian brokenness that I would grow accustomed to, yet never numb to in my heart. Every day it seemed that I passed at least 5 extremely drunken men on my short walk to the Claretian monastery to pray. Life in Russia was so bad that people often drank—they drank to forget, they drank from depression, they drank because they were cold (to 'keep warm'), and they drank because they were addicted. All the problems in Russia were an intertangled mess. They were alcoholics and when parents, live-in boyfriends or girlfriends, siblings or neighbors drank, children were often abused—sexually, physically, emotionally, and mentally. Almost all children in Russia suffer some sort of abuse—often sexual. Because people were abused as children, they abuse alcohol and other children when they become adults. Because people are abused and drink, there are no families. And because there are no families, people have no foundation for love or just good, fundamental childhood development, and therefore they do not ever want to get married or have kids. Instead, they fall into prostitution, have many abortions, and abuse alcohol and drugs (I still do not know where they got money for drugs, but I found used heroine needles on the sidewalk or in our apartment corridor often). On several occasions

---

[7] September 21, 2001

I found dead bodies (or dying people) on the streets—stepped over by the passersby. People were seemingly oblivious to other's pain, and too afraid to show love or help to their neighbor.

What I came to notice in the Russians was a general feeling of fear all the time. They feared everything and everyone—not only death, but also life. I think that what Communism did was instill this great fear in people in order to control them. I believe that this fear was also a result of the devil being so present in that country for so many years. The devil always brings fear, darkness, and confusion—where the presence of God frees a person in peace, light, and simple clarity. People in Russia were afraid to breathe wrong. Seriously. They had witnessed with their own eyes so much unjust, irrational suffering inflicted on innocent people that they feared somehow it would happen to them. They heard their neighbors awoken in the middle of the night by government officials, and they learned to not ask questions when loved ones 'disappeared,' often shipped off to the prisons without explanations. They had learned that if a person questioned that system, they also shortly after 'disappeared.' I remember one old lady telling me that she remembered when she was little being separated from her family and sent to work camps in Siberia when her father was arrested for being an 'enemy of the state.' And what was his crime? He owned a sewing machine—and the accusation was that obviously he was 'rich' and wanted to be better than the masses. People were often 'watched' during those dark years under Communism's reign, and no one felt secure and safe from unjust persecution. It could and did happen to anyone at any point for seemingly no reason whatsoever. This led people to be very leery of helping anyone else. If neighbors were in trouble, you shut your windows in order to not 'accidentally' hear. If someone was murdered and you witnessed it, you never reported it to the police, for they would write your name down in their books and that eventually meant problems for your family. This fear grew to a numb apathy about others' pain. And I witnessed that every day on the streets, where no one smiled at each other and no one said a word to each other on the public buses. On a few occasions, I found dead or dying people on the streets, and others stepped over them as if they had been trash on the ground. And when I stopped to help them, I was stared at as if I had come from another planet. My love was not understandable to them.

Another time in the spring of 2003, I traveled with a sister and priest to Irkutsk for the Chrism Mass at the Cathedral. As we walked from the train station and down the street, I noticed in an alleyway that there was an old, poor, sick man lying in the trash. I ran to him and called to sister and father, who quickly rushed to where I was hovering over this suffering soul. We were not sure if he was drunk or not, for he was so old that he shook all the time, and he was so weak that he could not speak nor stand. He was bleeding in a few places, and we were at a loss as to what to do to help him. We tried to help him walk back into the train station, for it was so cold outside, but in the end, we had to carry him because he was so weak that he could not walk. People stared at us as if we were crazy for helping such a poor and tattered man, and some even yelled things at us as we passed by. Once we brought him inside and found him a place to sit, sister went to call an ambulance to come and help him—for he was visibly hurt, as well as malnourished and frozen. Once the ambulance arrived, the female nurse walked over to us, and her face suddenly was transformed by anger. She said, "THIS is who you called us to help? THIS MAN? He is a man of the streets, a homeless man. We do not help creatures like him!" And she walked away and left. We were left at a loss as to what to do, for we could not just leave this dying man alone, but we had no place to take him. We went and bought some warm tea and a piece of bread and helped him to drink it and eat the bread dipped in it (he had no teeth and so could not chew). Then we found some other homeless people in the train station who seemed to know the man, and we turned him over to their care. I was amazed at how frozen people's hearts seemed toward this suffering, helpless man. Yet as I said before, the Russian people's fear turned into numb apathy and at times, hatred for their neighbor.

On one occasion I found myself in trouble, as some drunken young men were trying to break into my apartment to hurt me one night, and none of my neighbors would help me when they heard the pounding and screams of the men in the hallway. On another occasion, a man and his wife were gunned down in their apartment and their 10-month-old son (who witnessed this horror) cried alone until morning because the neighbors (who later admitted to hearing the gunshots and crying) were too afraid to call the police or help the frightened boy. Russians were afraid and they had learned to simply ignore the suffering of others around them. This sort of fear of everyone naturally leaked over into the Russian's spiritual life and relationship with God. And so, they also feared Him as a tyrant ready to condemn all who stepped the wrong way. I would come to find out that the only remedy for this deep sickness of fear would be Love—Jesus' Love both in the Eucharist and in a visible way around them in those in the Church who served them. For as St. John writes, *"Perfect Love casts out fear."*[8] And only His Love was perfect.

I was continually amazed at the great paradox that Russia seemed to be. In some ways, the people were much deeper and more real than the usual person from the West—for suffering had really stripped them from superficiality. I could have deeper, more serious conversations with some drunken men on the streets in Russia than with many worldly, 'happy,' and 'normal' people I knew in America. Yet on the other hand, although suffering had 'deepened' them in some ways, they had also become numb robots in other ways because of their great pain. I wrote home at the beginning of my second year in Siberia trying to explain some of these interesting characteristics I had found in the hearts of my brothers and sisters there. I think I explained my heart well in this letter, and so I will simply include a long excerpt from it here. I wrote:

Well, 'rainy season' has kicked in Krasnoyarsk....a few days ago, it suddenly cooled off and started raining. I guess that is it

---

[8] 1 John 4:18

for summer. Fall and spring are short. Rainy season is now here. Soon enough will be snow—and then freeze!!!

Rainy season in Krasnoyarsk means dirty season. You know, the Russians are a funny people—interesting, I guess, is a better word. In some ways, they are way underdeveloped. For example, rainy season in Krasnoyarsk is dirty season because we have no developed sewage systems. Every time it rains, everything floods. The little path we take up to the Claretian monastery everyday turns into a little river. And it is not just water—the whole sewage system backs up. It is amazing that they never thought up something like a sewage system for this big, 1,000,000-person governmental city. It is pretty yucky to walk through—we just try to take the high land and 'not look down.' Yet, on the other hand, the Russians are way more cultured than many in America are. Sister told me that the other day that she was walking with a young 23- or 24-year-old girl who was having a bad day, and this girl broke into famous Russian poetry to answer Sister's question of 'How are you?' And this is not uncommon. The simple lady that runs the corner store, or even the middle-aged drunk man on the path, often will recite famous Russian poets or philosophers in day-to-day conversation. To celebrate a 'victory' in AA, they often break into poetry or song over their tea, cookies and pastry. They are a living paradox in many ways.

Another example of the 'great Russian paradox' is that sometimes you can go to a village and find the most beautiful little houses with flower gardens and beehives. But, if you go to a Russian city, you see that there is almost no beauty....many tall, gray buildings in a row. That is it. On the retreat in Achinsk, one of the sisters from Poland asked me about this. Why, did I think, were the cities in Russia so ugly, dirty and covered in trash? As I pondered this, I thought of the relationship between God, Beauty, and Truth. The people in the villages often hid away a faith or belief in God in the bottom of their souls, and so Beauty was protected a bit, treasured in their hearts. In the cities, however, people lost the 'simple country life' and were quickly pulled into the work regime and Communist thought. When Communism took God from the people, they put work and productivity as priorities in place of His Love. Beauty comes from a heart in love. When a person loves, he tries to make himself beautiful for his beloved. He also tries to give beautiful things to his beloved. When God was cut from Russia's heart, they also lost Beauty. When you take God from a person, that person also ceases to seek Truth, the Truth of his dignity, and the Truth of His God's Love as reflected in Beauty. In this state, creation is not treasured, nurtured, or loved. Creation has no dignity. Life has no Beauty. The human person takes in information, but not 'Truth'...Truth is knowledge as seen in the Light of God. Truth is information that has a living meaning as it points to the Beauty of our Creator's Love....Truth, Beauty, God- They are all connected. When God is absent in a soul, there is no inspiration to live....life turns into a mechanical game of survival.

This I have seen really clearly in conversations with people over the last year. Just last week, I had two conversations with a church-going young woman who actually said to me, "Why do I have to believe in God? Why can't I just exist and live my day-to-day life like those people over there on the street?" She had no inspiration to seek Love, Truth, Beauty...something more than pure existence. Anytime I used the word 'heart' in our conversation, she said, *"I don't know what you are talking about... 'heart'. I don't have a 'heart'. I have a mind. I can think; I have feelings...but what is this 'heart?' I think and I feel...period."* And I know that this young woman has suffered much in her life, without God. And therefore, her heart is so wounded, closed, and afraid, that talk about God giving meaning to suffering meant nothing. Jesus' Heart pierced open on the Cross to her was a bad feeling Jesus suffered and made no sense. She was afraid of relationships, afraid to love, afraid of so much.....and so even if one could reason with her about God's existence, it was hard for her to take a step of 'faith.' *"What is this faith, belief?"* she would ask me. *"I think and I feel...period."* The beautiful thing is that because she has 'nothing better to do' she comes to Mass almost daily, leads the rosary often, helps the sisters, even comes to Adoration often....and cries through it all. I know that through a living encounter with Jesus' Eucharistic Heart, and the Immaculate Heart of Mary in the rosary, her heart is being opened whether she likes it or not. She keeps coming; she keeps asking. And as God enters her life, so does Love, so does Beauty, so does

Truth. She receives a little more from God each day and asks fewer questions. The 'information' she receives from a homily at Mass I see her live. If she begins to live Jesus' 'information', than she begins to live Truth, in the Light, with God. And so, His Love starts to drip between the cracks of her heart. And this Great Love of His will heal her. Her problem is not rare; I think many in Russia have 'lost their heart', because they have lost God. And when a person loses his heart, he loses his very self. Yet, God is the 'Divine Chess Player'. He is always finding a new way 'in'. The Russian Heart, lost because Jesus had been lost, has cracked from its dry thirst....and through these cracks He will enter. He does enter.

On my train-ride into Russia the first time I was here (in 1994), a SOLT priest explained an important thing to me about the Russian Heart. He said that there is a huge difference between the Russian Heart and an American Heart. He said that the problem in America is that our hearts have grown cold and hard. We have Jesus in many churches and many opportunities to meet with Him every day—we have the freedom to follow His Laws. And what we have done is turned from Him. We have allowed our hearts to turn cold to His Love (in many ways), and therefore they have hardened in pride. In Russia, the people have wounded hearts. They had God 'stolen' from them, and they were victims of many years of atheistic darkness. They have been wounded deeply....crucified without Jesus. And the Cross without God is hell. And so, as their wounded hearts—which are afraid to open, trust, receive or give love- crack open in sores, God can enter. And He does. They have good intentions many times, but are just so wounded....they can't meet God and so don't see or live Truth. They have wounded hearts, and so they have 'buried' them and our Living God within them deep inside. Their hearts are closed from fear- but love can heal wounds and open them. (Just as His Love and Mercy is trying to soften and open our hearts in the West.) And so that, I believe, is the deepest apostolic need in Russia- to help the people find their heart, and live from their heart with God.

The Catholic Catechism states that the *"...heart is the dwelling place where I am, where I live...it is our hidden center, beyond the grasp of our reason and of others; only the Spirit of God can fathom the human heart and know it fully. The heart is the place of decision, deeper than our psychic drives. It is the place of truth, where we choose life or death. It is the place of encounter, because as image of God we live in relation: it is the place of covenant."* (2563) It also states, *" Whether prayer is expressed in words or gestures, it is the whole man who prays. But in naming the source of prayer, Scripture speaks sometimes of the soul or the spirit, but most often of the heart (more than a thousand times.) According to Scripture, it is the heart that prays. If our heart is far from God, the words of prayer are in vain."* (2562) If a human heart is the sanctuary of God, beyond reason, only understood by Him, our Creator, than when a person loses God, they also lose a part of themselves, the deepest part of themselves that enables them to love. This is the problem in Russia.

The Russian people live on a very emotional level, intellectual level in some respects. Yet, this is only because God was stolen from them in the time of Communism, and therefore, they lost their heart. Without a relationship with God to draw them deep into their beings, without prayer (which comes from the heart), their heart grew very far from themselves. God never left His people.... He waits in their hearts for their return. He quietly whispers; and in the moments when mind and emotion fail these blessed people, they hear the echo of God's voice deep within. God uses their wounds to heal them. And that is why Adoration of Jesus' Heart is so important here. His Heart's Love will awaken their hearts. And that is why Mary has chosen the Russian land as a special place of conversion for Her Heart's Triumph. Her Heart communes with God in the midst of Her chosen Russian people, for Her children in

Russia, and Her Heart will teach them again about their own heart. She will teach them about God's Love, Beauty, and the Truth, Who is Her Son, dwelling in Her Heart. She will help them find their 'sanctuary, where God is dwelling within' again. It is all so amazing to me. Because I see all this incarnated into our everyday life here…in the midst of the 'B-grade movie,' God is working in a very profound way.[9]

And that was the sad reality of Russia. There were beautiful treasures that Jesus was to show me inside all of that mess, yet the fact that the society was a mess was simple truth. I loved them, but I suffered for them, with them, from them. I felt such a pain in my heart on a daily basis for them—for Jesus allowed me to feel their pain in my heart. And in light of all their problems, sins, sufferings

[9] Excerpt from my Newsletter 23, August 26 2002

and wounds, I understood that the *only* solution to save them was Jesus. Russia needs a Savior—as we all need a Savior. As the people of Russia come to know Jesus, allow Him to draw close and love them, then He will be able to heal them and all of Russia's wounds from the inside out. Yet the people are so unfamiliar with God that they need to meet Him living *in* others. And that is why Russia so needs missionaries.

Chapter 4

A Place of Darkness, A Place of Miracles

"How can he call this place miraculous?" the young missionary sister asked me. *"I just don't understand him."* This question was part of a conversation I had once with a young sister new to her mission in Siberia. She sat across from me at the kitchen table in her community's apartment-monastery. She stared at me with big, sad, brown eyes open wide in shock as we discussed the many problems that faced the people she had recently began serving. The 'he' she was referring to in our conversation was another

missionary priest—a man I had worked closely with during my 2 years serving in the Krasnoyarsk area. He was a very holy man, a man who had given most of his priesthood to this mission in Siberia. This sister was recalling to me over our morning coffee together a conversation she had recently had with this Claretian father. He had told her how she must simply fall in love with Russia—that was the only way to help her—and he told her that when she fell in love with the people, she would see that this land of darkness was truly a place of miracles. The struggle that this sister faced was a normal one for a new missionary to Siberia. When one arrives for the first time he can be surprised, even shocked, that the reality of difficulties in life for the normal Siberian person greatly surpass what their imaginations may have prepared themselves for. Yes, as I explained in previous chapters, there are many levels of suffering, of evil, of problems in Russia. Yet, it is also true that God reaches into this darkness and does place His Light… He does make miracles.

An Unexpected Meeting…

One such miracle story happened to me on my flight into Russia on my way to Siberia in June, 2001. I clearly remember the landing of the plane in Moscow's airport that spring morning. As we began to descend, I felt this rush of darkness come over me and a pit grew in my stomach. Someone had arranged for some sisters to meet me at the airport to help me transfer to another airport for my next flight, yet I did not know how I would find them or what I was supposed to do to get through customs (and my lack of knowledge of the Russian languages did not help much either). There seemed to be a thick veil of evil I felt each time I entered Russia, a suffocating darkness—and each time I was to leave Russia, I would feel this cloud become lifted. I prayed, "*Oh Mother, this is Your land, please help me. Help me find my way, help the sisters be there. Oh, I trust in You, my Mother, I trust in You.*" I specifically felt from these first moments of darkness that Mary in a particular way wanted to be my help, protection, and guide. God had entrusted Russia to Her in a special way in Fatima, and I was only coming to be the physical 'hands' of Her Heart's work there.

As we began to get off the plane, the most amazing thing happened. I spotted someone on the plane that I actually knew. Seven years earlier when I had worked in Moscow for the summer, I had traveled there with a Bishop from Slovakia who helped to form the community in which I was volunteering. I actually had a friend in SOLT who had told me in America that she knew him, and she gave me his home phone number and address to contact him when I was visiting in Rome (where he was living at that time) on my way to Russia. She had many spiritual gifts and felt that I needed his blessing. Well, I did not have the courage to contact him in Rome, and I did not want to bother the sisters in trying to help me find him, so I never called. I even saw his secretary on the street outside of a church one day, and I felt like that was Jesus' way of nudging me to call the Bishop. Yet, in the end I just did not do it. And so here, climbing off my plane from Rome in Moscow, I thought I spotted him. I doubted myself, for I had not seen him or had any sort of contact in seven years with any of those people with whom I had worked that summer. Yet I was sure in the heart of my heart that it was him. This gave me hope. He was waiting for everyone else to get off the plane before he found his way off. I walked slowly, looking behind me. I had decided that maybe I would ask his help to get through the airport. Russian customs and airports are very difficult to travel through, and I did not know exactly how to do it. As I stood in line to go through the little border patrol table, I saw walk down the stairs behind me not only this Bishop, but a priest as well. This priest had been the priest in charge of our whole 40+ people group training into Moscow the summer when I was seventeen, for he was sort of the overseer of all the missions in Russia for this community. He knew English well and actually had been the person who put me on the plane to leave Moscow at the end of my summer stay there seven years before. It was my turn to go through passport control as I realized who they were, and so I waited on the other side for them. I approached this priest (who was traveling with another priest in addition to the Bishop) and reintroduced myself, asking me if he remembered me. He smiled very big and said that of course he remembered me. He introduced me to the Bishop again, who gave me his little blessing (in a secret little way) there in the airport. I felt like I received new strength as I received this holy Bishop's blessing in the dark airport. This priest helped me find my bags and fill out the custom forms, which were in Russian. Then he told me that if I went through the second customs table, that waiting on the other side of the doors for them would be a religious sister in her white habit. I was so excited! This sister had been the sister who was in charge of the mission in Moscow when I had been there seven years earlier, and she often came to visit and care for my friend and I when we were in Gagarinka. She, too, had come with this priest to put us on the plane when I had last left Moscow to return home, and I was overwhelmed by the great Love Jesus gave me in having these friends 'waiting' for me there when I arrived again. When I went out, this sister remembered my face immediately, and we hugged. I told her that some sisters were supposed to be meeting me, but we could not find them, and I did not have much time to change airports before my next flight. She felt badly that she could not drive me, for her car was already full with the Bishop, two priests, and their suitcases. Yet, she found me a good taxi that only wanted $30.00 to drive me between the airports. Sister gave me her phone number and address in Moscow and told me if I ever needed help when I traveled through again, to please just call her. And I did use this help many times in the future. Sister said that she felt like Jesus must have really wanted her to pray for me if we reunited so mysteriously after so many years. And we began to pray for each other in a special way that day.

I might as well add here another amazing bit of information. The second priest traveling with the Bishop—whom I did not think that I knew—was also placed on my path by God. Seven months after this meeting in Moscow, I would travel to Poland with one of my spiritual Russian sisters for a one-month retreat. As we stopped in Moscow and called this sister, she arranged for us to be picked up and to stay the night at an apartment set up specifically for missionaries traveling through Moscow on the way to their various missions throughout Russia. When I arrived that February on my way back from Poland, there was a priest staying at the apartment indefinitely to sort of look after and care for the missionaries—as well as to do some work for the Bishop. At this point, I could speak Russian fairly well, and as this priest began speaking with me, I found out that he was the priest traveling with the Bishop that day I met them in the Moscow airport. He remembered me. And, even more interesting, he also was with me seven years earlier at the retreat in Slovakia and traveling into Moscow. Not only did he remember me, but as we talked, I began to remember him. We had been in the same place at the same time three times in our lives, yet we never could communicate until that February afternoon because only at that point had we both learned Russian. (He was from Brazil or Chile, I don't remember exactly—but he spoke Spanish). We were from the same half of the world and had been together on several occasions, but God waited until we were both in Moscow to allow us to communicate through the Russian language that we both were learning little by little. This meeting was so mysterious (and what many would call 'coincidental'— although I see it as providential), that I decided God really must have wanted our lives intertwined, and I began to pray for him as well. The world is so small in the body of Christ—and we are so connected by His precious Blood. We breathe the same faith, and so it makes sense that God so closely intertwines our lives in His Son.

"I have called you by name, you are Mine..."—Isaiah 43:1

Not only did God move so profoundly among the missionaries who came to serve Him in Russia, but He also directly reached into the darkness of Communist, atheist Russia to 'steal' His precious children back to His Love. The greatest miracle stories I know from Russia have to do with one Russian sister and one Russian priest. The priest grew up in a traditional soviet family. His father was an influential member of the soviet army and party, as well as his grandparents. His mother was a theatre director. And no one in his family believed in God. When he was young and asked about God existing, he was punished. His family was Communist, and Lenin was their god. When this priest was a young boy, his father was sent on an assignment to East Germany. Their family was given special permission to live and roam freely among the Germans in the section of Berlin where they lived. It was during this time that this priest first found a Catholic Church. He had a mystical experience in front of a statue of Our Lady (although he was only 7 years old and, mind you, from a staunch atheist, Communist family), and from that seed his priesthood began to grow. There are many miracle stories which led to his eventual conversion and ordination, but I think that his priesthood itself is the greatest miracle of all. Mary reached her hand down into the depths of darkness—into the 'pit' of an atheist, Communist family—and said, 'I want him.' He is today a very holy priest.

The second miracle story is of a friend of mine, a Russian religious sister. She was raised in a good home, yet without the strong faith of the Catholic Church. She worked for many years for the Communist party herself, until finally one day her conscience began to speak to her telling her that she should not continue with the work for moral reasons. She was not affiliated with any church at that time yet did leave her work causing a great scandal because of her high position. Eventually, God led her to the Catholic Church, and after many years of struggle and searching and healing she finally became a religious sister. Today, she serves in the very Siberian city where she was born, and she has a powerful prayer ministry.

And so, although Russia is a place of great darkness, of evil and sufferings on every human level, there are great graces present there. The challenge is to look at Jesus being crucified in Russia and to find His Hope, His Light, His beauty and grace within the thorns of the Cross' night. It is precisely in the suffering and dark places that God comes to give life, to give hope. It was in the suffering that I found the face of my crucified Jesus. The following are simply snippets of stories of various people I encountered during my time in Russia. Some of these stories simply show Russia's poverty and how Jesus' face can be found within such dire situations. But most of them show how God reached into this poor darkness and kissed His people with Love. They are miracle stories that took place in the darkness. Sometimes, the miracle is simply that in the depths of such atheist pain, God would reach down and place Love. He would do this through a person or mission. Often, the service that missionaries gave in Russia changed them to be much holier. Russia is the place of deeper conversion for many people who visit in order to help. It is a place of spiritual renewal because a missionary must be renewed spiritually in order to endure. It was miraculous for me that Jesus would allow me to so intimately touch His wounded face within the wounds of my brothers and sisters whom I met there. Truly I learned, *"That which you do to the least of my brothers, you did unto me..."* *(Matthew 25:40)*

A Homeless Babushka

One of the first visible ways I met Jesus' poverty on the Cross in

my Russian sisters and brothers happened one Sunday morning as Sister and I walked to Mass. We often left for Mass early so that we had a little extra time to do 'beggar ministry.' We never wanted to just give people money, even if they were hungry and that is all they wanted. We desired to give them love, more than anything, and the hope of God. We would place a 5- or 10-ruble coin in the dirty, plastic cup they took from the nearby trash in which they collected money. Yet we would also ask their name and we would speak to them about God's Love for them. Each situation was different, and so we especially prayed to the Holy Spirit to help guide us so that our words would touch their hearts. This morning, Jesus gave to me much more than I could give to the old babushka I met—for He gave me her suffering in my heart in a special way, and through that I came to understand His suffering with the Russian people better. About 15 minutes from the church, we met this beautiful, old, old, old babushka begging. We stopped to talk to her, and she broke down crying, saying over and over again in muddled Russian that when she was little someone came and took her mother and father, that she was left alone and scared and that she prayed and prayed. She might have been speaking about a haunting memory she had from her childhood, yet to her the pain was as real as if it had

happened that very morning. She could not hear at all, and so we could not ask her questions in order to understand her story better. She just cried and cried. We did understand that she was hungry, and so we went to buy some soft bread (because she had no teeth) and water for her. When we brought it to her, she tried to give us back the little coin we had given her as payment. We placed it back in her little cup as we knelt down to feed her (as she was too weak to feed herself). I held the water and handed Sister pieces of wet bread, which she held up to the mouth of our old sister. After she ate enough, we placed the bread and water near her, knowing that she could not carry it herself, but hoping that someone would come for her and take it with them for her. When we gave her a miraculous medal, she pulled out from beneath her bundle of clothes a cross and she let us pray with her. And as she was pretty calm again, we hurriedly continued walking to Mass (for at this point we were running late). This woman's face and heart are etched in the memory of my heart until today. She is probably the poorest woman I have ever met. She had no home, food, or love. My heart hurt that morning that we could not help her more than we had. Yet, we had nothing more to give her, not even a listening ear because she could not hear and she was unable to communicate too much. I had to believe that our love, even if it was only for a few moments, somehow eased her life's pain. Sister and I tried to be very conscious of not falling into the trap of just pitying her in a condescending way, but instead truly loving her and respecting her dignity and life. We tried to love her as an equal, as a friend; for truly she was our sister, and the beloved of Jesus' Heart.

Brothers and Sisters on the Streets

As I said before, Sister and I loved to do our 'beggar ministry,' and we met some really interesting people. I quickly learned that unlike America, when people are begging on the streets, they usually really needed food, shelter, or clothes. During Communism, a person's basic needs were always cared for by the state. Yet as that foundation was pulled out from under the Russian people, and as it was not replaced by a good foundation of democracy and capitalism, people simply fell into the ground and were buried in hunger and economic problems. Even well-educated Russians had great difficulty finding a job. And life was so depressing and seemingly hopeless in these people's great suffering that people turned heavily to drinking, drugs and suicide. Although Sister and I tried to help all those we met on the streets, we had to be careful how we helped them. People who seemed to have tendencies to alcoholism (people whom we met who were drunk, for example) we would not give money. Yet we would try to give bread and milk to anyone who asked. I remember on our first little walk through Irkutsk the day after I arrived in Russia, we met a middle-aged drunken man, who stopped us to talk because of Sister's habit. He cried about his life to us and told us how he felt guilty about his alcoholism, but that he felt helpless to help himself. We promised to pray for him, as he begged us not for money, but instead only for spiritual help. We also met that day a lady on the street who asked us for a piece of clothing, as she only had one dress, and it was ripped. A little later that day Sister was approached by a little group of dirty street boys asking for bread. When she came away from the nearby kiosk and handed the bread to them, they tore it to pieces in front of her and quickly gobbled it all up. Sister told me that once she had heard a voice coming from inside the sewer drain on the street in the winter. There was a man freezing to death down there (he had climbed in it because it was warmer than the minus-40-degree weather outside) who begged for help and food. The suffering around me seemed to be endless between the stories I heard and the faces my eyes met. But no matter how deep the darkness was around me, there was a place for God's Love to enter in and transform these situations. Dire suffering and poverty always has a place for a miracle of God's Love—whether it be supernatural intervention or simply God loving the poor through another person He created. One thing I learned in Russia was that no matter how dark a situation may be, God's light is shining underneath it—you simply have to scratch away the dirt and dust of this world clouding His presence over.

I remember one beggar lady I met, Ekateria (Catherine), who was an older babushka. She actually was very well educated. It was obvious by the way she held herself and how she spoke. In talking with her I came to know that she could read and write in a few different languages. Yet here she was, out of work and begging on the street for food. She had no one to help her and left alone in life and aging, she had no means of receiving or making money. What I remember most about her was that she was joyful. I felt that she had to be close to God, to be in such bad straights and still find reason to smile. Most of the people whom Sister and I met were very depressed and hungry for love. They would just look at us and start crying because they could not believe we stopped to ask their name and to talk to them. They rarely met simple kindness on the streets. One day sister met a very old man sitting with his empty cup begging, holding an accordion. Sister later related to me that she stopped to give him money one day, but instead of just walking on quickly, she sat down next to him and asked him to play music for her. Of course, the man could not play very well (for he was so old and his hands shaky), but sister wanted to give him more than money through her request—she wanted to give him dignity. She wanted him to think that his music was beautiful and important to someone—that he was beautiful and important to someone.

Some Hungry Girls

Although it was heartbreaking for me to meet these beggars on the street, nothing tore at my heart more than the great suffering of children I saw everywhere around me. Jesus taught me about the poverty they suffered in not only a lack of food, of a home, of family, but a poverty of love in their lives—especially the sort of Love His presence brings. These children's hearts I met not only on the streets or when we traveled to the villages, but I encountered a few of them very closely right in our monastery dining room. One such incident happened one evening about a month after I arrived in Krasnoyarsk. At midnight one evening, I heard the doorbell. I waited for one of the priests to answer it, as our neighbor sold illegal alcohol and often drunk men accidentally rang our door looking for their house. But this night Jesus brought us a treasure. As I sat at the dining room table writing in my journal and drinking a cup of tea, I heard a bunch of footsteps come up the stairs to the entrance of the monastery. The priest who had answered the door had let somebody in, and I was really surprised when their faces appeared in the doorway. Standing hesitatingly near our front corridor were four visibly poor, young girls (between 10-15 years old). They knew that priests lived there, and they were really hungry. They came simply to beg for food. And I think that they were shocked that Father did not simply give them bread, but instead warmly welcomed them into the house and hurried to the kitchen to heat up soup leftover from lunch. They were visibly embarrassed at having to beg. And except for the spunky 10-year-old girl named Masha, they sat silent. With a little coaxing they began to talk, as I tried in my broken Russian to make them feel at home while they waited for father and the soup. When he finally did bring it out, they scarfed it down quickly, and he offered them seconds. When we put honey on the table to go in their tea, little Masha took her spoon and ate spoonful after spoonful straight from the bowl. She did not think anyone noticed. I thought of how embarrassing it would be to have to beg for food at your neighbors whom you did not know. All I could think was, *"God bless the children of Russia. We truly do not appreciate what we have in the U.S."* It gave me great joy to see how hard Father worked to not only feed their tummies, but also to bring smiles back to their faces.

A Teenage Orphan

Right around the same time as the previous incident, Jesus brought a little boy into my heart at the same dining room table. He had come to stay at the monastery for a few days. He was 14 years old, but physically very small as he was sickly. He had been in the hospital in Krasnoyarsk, and when he was released, he had needed somewhere to stay until a religious sister could come from his city to take him back there on the train. His parents had been killed a few years earlier,

and although he had a 24-year-old sister who had custody over him, she lived with some man and did not care to look after her younger brother. I asked one of the Russian sisters from his city about him, and she said, "I'm his only mother." He had actually begged her to take legal custody of him, but as she needed to be faithful to her religious vocation, she was unable to. Yet, she tried to mother him as much as she could, helping him out when he found himself in need. He often got into trouble when left unattended, but with a little love he dissolved into a holy little boy. I spent lots of time looking at books and reading with him. He felt smart as he could help me with my poor Russian, explaining proper pronunciation of words. He cried and cried, hugging onto my waist for a good minute or two when he left, and he promised to pray every day that I could stay in Russia forever. I would come to see that lots of children lived in similar situations without family and without love. I know that that is why my Jesus asked His Mother to specially take Russia under Her care—He saw the land of the motherless, where many women had forgotten what it meant to love a child—and He sent His Mother to teach them through Her love of Her Son. Mary's gentle Love, especially of Jesus' wounded Heart on the Cross, would truly be the only hope for many of the children in Russia. Through Her love of Him *for* them,

they would receive the grace to know and love Him themselves again.

Retreats for Children

About a month after I arrived in Siberia for the first time a sister invited me to come and help on a vacation Bible school she was going to have for about 20 children for 2 weeks. I had to travel with a priest for 1 ½ hours to reach their mission. When we arrived in the afternoon this Sister was waiting for me at the little retreat center they had there.  I had no idea what was in store for me this week. Children started arriving, and before I knew it there were about 20 of them ranging in ages from 5-13 or so. Sister was all by herself, and she pulled me aside and said to me, "I have to go do something. Take the kids and talk to them or something until I get back. Teach them a game so that they get to know each other." I said, "Sister, I don't speak Russian." And she said, "Oh, don't worry. Just think of something until I return. Sing with them or tell them about America." And she left me for 45 minutes with a circle of kids sitting on the floor around me. I laughed to myself and thought, *"This sister is crazy. How in the world am I supposed to entertain so many kids—'tell them about America' or 'sing with them' if I DON'T SPEAK THE LANGUAGE?"* But that was my dear Sister. And I quickly learned Russian that week, precisely because she did put me in such situations. I learned it from necessity and from her love. As I sat in that circle with the kids, I tried to speak with them, and they laughed at my poor Russian and tried to guess what I wanted to say. In the end, I took out my guitar and figured that if I could not sing Russian songs with them, I would just teach them the Russian songs they already knew, but in English. They LOVED that! And so I found myself, tucked away in a little Siberian city, singing all the

praise songs I loved from my years at Notre Dame—with a choir of Russian children's voices accompanying me out of tune, but with good American accents. The funniness of the whole situation struck me, and I laughed in joy at Jesus' sense of humor in putting me in such precarious situations.

Each child at this bible camp had his own sad life story. Some of these children had never stepped into a church in their entire life. Others had never been out of their little village, and so busses and trolleys were an exciting (and sometimes dangerous) novelty to them. None of them had been around so much love and mothering before that week, as this was Sister's first year of doing a Bible camp—and these children came from very broken homes. Many of the kids either did not have parents or did not have parents who cared for them. Some ran on the streets; others lived with grandparents. Some of the kids came without underwear, shoes, or a change of clothes. And so Sister and I ran out one afternoon to get the basics so that the kids could be clean, clothed, and comfortable (and not embarrassed in front of the other children.) There was one little boy who was mentally handicapped and very poorly behaved. He and his sister traveled to Achinsk for this retreat from their little village (to which the sisters and priest traveled to celebrate Mass once every two weeks.) Their parents were severe alcoholics, and the children were left to do as they pleased. If they were hungry, they somehow had to find something to eat themselves. The parents received some special money from the government to help educate the little boy who was sick, but they used that money for vodka. Some kind parish ladies offered to

keep him and get him into special schools, but the parents were always too drunk to sign the necessary forms. He told us how he had to find potatoes himself and boil them for food. He was very mentally and emotionally sick, but he responded very energetically to love. All the children were hungry for love. And so, every morning each one ran to me for hugs and kisses as soon as they woke up. There was one little boy from the neighboring parish whose mother had died, and he wanted for me to be his new mom. He was about 12 or so, and he shyly fell in love with me, I think. I felt such deep suffering in his heart over his mom. And every time I saw him after that, I felt the same suffering. I feel his suffering now, as I write. And so, I took him as a special spiritual son, and I gave him to Mary, and I prayed for him often. There was another little girl who fell in love with one of the priests when he came to visit for a couple of days during those two weeks. She did not have a father herself, and she decided that she wanted Father to be her dad. When he left one day to celebrate the Masses in the villages, she cried and cried. She was only 6 years old, but she refused to eat or get out of bed. She was lovesick. Eventually, we somehow coaxed her to get up and play with the rest of the children. I truly loved these children—they were so lost, and so dear to God's Heart. I spent a lot of time those two weeks playing ball, coloring, singing with them and praying with them. It was a very beautiful experience.

The most beautiful part of the whole two weeks with the children was on Saturday night, when we gathered in the church for four hours of adoration, praise, and worship before Jesus in the Blessed Sacrament. The kids were told that they did not have to stay (they could go to bed), but most of them did stay the whole time. Sister asked me if I would pray with her over each child and, of course, I agreed with joy. The way we prayed with the children that evening was thus: we had each child come up and kneel before the monstrance while we placed our hands on their heads and prayed with them. We asked them each what they wanted to pray for, and their answers astonished me. For not knowing God, their hearts so purely sought, believed, trusted, and loved Him. They were not perfect, but they were sincere. They poured out their hearts to Jesus that night asking for faith for their unbelieving parents, for healing from their parents' alcoholism, for the gift of prayer and being good. Each one cried and cried as we prayed over them. Some later approached Sister and asked, "Why did I cry when we prayed? I didn't want to." One of the little boys was really touched when I prayed in tongues over him. He later came up

to me and asked, "Sister,[10] what were you saying when you prayed over me? What kind of prayer was that? It was neat." The whole experience was really powerful. Some adults from the parish were also there and came up for prayer. All in all, many beautiful seeds of Christ's Love were planted. And I prayed that those seeds would somehow blossom in the midst of the big spiritual war I saw around me.

---

[10] Everyone in Russia called me 'sister,' even though I was a lay missionary. Although I would sometimes explain the difference to the adults, they did not really understand. And so, I allowed and answered to 'sister,' thinking that it was a good example to them of how we are all brothers and sisters. I also tried to teach them in it how a natural sister should love.

A Russian Marriage

It was funny on the Friday of that week when Sister approached me, telling me that a couple was going to get married in the church that afternoon (which was a new idea in Russia, unheard of by many people), and asking me to play music with the kids at the wedding. Now I was wearing jeans and a ripped t-shirt, and my other clothes were back at the sisters' monastery where I was staying. Yet my clothes seemed to be completely irrelevant to Sister. I agreed to play, but I laughed to myself thinking of me (with my simple, poor guitar skills), in my poor clothes sitting in a back of this little mobile home style church playing Russian music (in my broken Russian) with a bunch of ragamuffin kids singing for a wedding. I was not the only amateur at the wedding, for a priest had arrived to help out at the retreat for a few days, and

Sister grabbed him last minute to celebrate the wedding Mass. The only thing was that he also did not know Russian well, and so he hurriedly  needed to practice reading the vows with the help of the children correcting his pronunciation. They had fun 'practicing' marrying each other. It was even funnier at the end when the TV stations and newspapers showed up, thinking it an interesting story that someone would get married in a church (since sacramental marriages were a new concept in Russia). I prayed that they did not get me in any footage during the wedding, yet afterwards I was pulled by Sister to be in some wedding pictures with the bride and groom (since I was American—something interesting to them—and because I had done the music). I was proud of this couple, who courageously wanted to embrace a sacramental marriage and who wanted to try to be open to children (when most Russians were afraid to have children considering their difficult economic and social problems). I took this couple as my spiritual children along with my little guys, for I knew that they would need lots of grace to grow in God, especially in the midst of such a still atheist culture. All in all, it was in situations like that wedding where I enjoyed

God the most—for I truly loved my mission life there, although I could hardly believe some of the things He asked me to do.

Praying Evil Away on the Trans-Siberian Railroad

Sister and I often had to ride the trains back and forth from Kansk my second year in Russia because the priest who went with us to the mission did not always have a car. The trips home on Sunday evenings were particularly bad, for the trains were squished with students returning to Krasnoyarsk for school (after visiting home on the weekend). There often was no place to sit for our 5-hour ride and it was very hot and very loud. These trips always made me very sick. One Sunday evening, Sister and I had a very close encounter with evil on the train, yet Jesus was very close to us. We had to sit across from a loud group of college kids who were obviously very far from God. Their conversation was very dark as well as obnoxious for most of our trip. At one point, one of the girls said that she was going to do white magic for the others—she was going to read their futures. She told them to write something down about themselves on a paper and she would tell them about their pasts and futures. When sister and I heard this, we looked at each other. I said to her, "Let's just pray a rosary silently," and we began to invoke the presence of Our Lady, all the Angels and Saints, as well as Jesus and the Holy Spirit. We prayed about half a rosary and the girl 'reading' the future of the others suddenly got mad. She yelled, "This is not working! You guys are not taking me seriously. You are joking at me and I cannot do it!" She was so upset that something was 'blocking' her magic that she got up and ran to a different train car in tears. After she left, all of her friends started making fun of the evil she was trying to do. And so, I saw in that the real hand of God trying to protect these unknowing college students from getting involved too deeply in such evil things. The whole time that this was going on I felt in my heart and sensibilities a little war between good and evil going on. I felt the strong presence of evil, but I also felt as if Jesus was very strongly present with me, with His arms wrapped in Love around my heart.

A Gypsy Child

Another day I encountered a different face of evil on the streets. I was walking to church for Mass, and I had stopped to buy myself an ice cream cone on the way. Yet, when I turned the corner, there sat two gypsy ladies with several naked children running wild around them. They were begging for money. I gave something little to them, as my heart was broken for the lives they were forced to live. I knew that many of these women were beaten by their alcoholic 'husbands' or 'masters' when they returned back home to the gypsy camps if they did not have enough money from begging. My heart always ached for them when I saw them, for they were raised in an atmosphere where they were taught abuse, lying, cheating, stealing, and many other sinful ways. I even had prayed that God would begin a religious order simply with the charism of serving these people, for they needed deep catechism and love of God to turn from their lifestyles. As I walked by the ladies, one of her children—maybe 3 or 4 years old—ran up to me and begged me for my ice cream cone. I did not hesitate a second, as I bent down and handed it to him. His mother felt bad and tried to apologize, and I smiled and said that it was fine—I was happy to give it to him. (I wondered how often, if ever, he ate ice cream.) Yet as I stood up from handing him my little gift, two big mafia looking, well-dressed men were standing before me laughing. They began to mock me for giving the child my food, and they began to yell impure things at me as well about 'giving them a little something.' They began to yell to others standing in the street, "Hey, did you see that lady?! She's got a soft heart!!! She gave her ice cream to them? Hey, lady, do you know what kind of trash they are?" As I walked past these men, I simply said to them, "They are children of God. They are my brothers and sisters." The men continued to laugh and yell profane things at me, and so I hurried away. Yet, my heart felt worse for the gypsy ladies and children, for they were left behind to continue to hear such degrading comments, and I knew that their lives were full of pure suffering.

A Black Street Dog

Another day I had an encounter with evil of a natural kind. As I walked out of my apartment to head down to the monastery chapel to pray, a huge, black dog came running and barking at me. I was sure he was going to bite me. As he jumped up at me, I immediately said, "In the name of Jesus Christ!" This seemingly funny response was from a habit I had whenever I encountered a situation of fear or evil. In such situations, I would automatically say, "In the name of Jesus Christ, satan be gone!" Well, this dog jumping at me with mouth open scared me, and I immediately screamed in English the beginning of this saying. I had just finished saying 'Christ' when suddenly the dog stopped in mid-air and fell to the ground laying there docile and ignoring me. This situation was an obvious witness to me of the power of Jesus' name.

Schools of Prayer

Although God's hand was obviously present in such extraordinary circumstances, Sister and I also witnessed His miraculous Love in all of our simple, ordinary, everyday lives. Besides devoting our time to learning the Russian language in our

first months in Krasnoyarsk, Sister and I quickly became involved in helping out with a number of activities in our parish. Our apartment became the host of many different parish groups several nights a week. The pastor at the parish asked Sister and I to begin a prayer group one evening a week. Immediately when Father asked us to do this and I prayed about it, Jesus showed me a very clear plan as to what these groups needed to be—not just prayer groups, but instead 'schools of prayer.' I explained why they needed to be 'schools of prayer' in a letter I wrote home on September 21, 2001:

These aren't just prayer groups, but 'Schools of Prayer.' To understand why, you must know a little background on the Russians: From Communism, Russians became very confused and were wounded in their hearts—many simply can't pray. It sounds strange, but it is just true. I have had many a Russian in tears in my arms because they 'just don't know how to pray.' It's interesting that when I've prayed with Russians and asked what they wanted to pray for, they ALWAYS say for FAITH. Here their lives are horrible, but all they want is FAITH—for themselves, for their families—even little kids of 5 or 6 ask for Faith (second and third place goes to Hope and Love believe it or not—they often add these to their requests for faith.) They know that faith will help them pray, but they say that they 'don't know how to get it.' (I had a man ask me the other day how he could have faith—did he just need to say a prayer? Did it have to be in Russian? If he did it in German, could he still 'get faith'?)

And so, this priest thought Sister and I could start a school for those who wanted to learn to pray.

I prayed about this idea, and the Holy Spirit made very clear to me one word: HEART. This was to be a school of the heart, which is the place where a person meets with God. The heart is a place many of these people do not know they have. And so, I began simple teachings on the heart—from the Catechism and the Bible. I planned to teach them about the Sacred Heart of Jesus (especially in the Eucharist) and the Immaculate Heart of Mary. Russians are very contemplative, deep people naturally (they may be disposed to this from their sufferings—life is serious, no one has time for superficiality). And so, I thought that by helping them find their heart and their God who lives within them (and by helping them know the Heart of God—the place in which they live) the Holy Spirit would be able to more easily carry them into contemplative prayer. They had been wounded so much that band-aids on their life problems did not help—the root of their problems (their heart) needed to be healed. They needed their heart and their heart's wounds to meet Jesus' Heart. For when they could see that He took their wounds onto His own Heart for them, then they would open to Him and His love would be able to heal, annihilate their pasts, and help them be born again in His resurrected love. I explained this in a letter I wrote home:

The Russian heart has to have its wounds burned away by the blood of Jesus—it is the only way to heal. For example, when I came, I was told the average woman has had 12 abortions. I have come to find out from Russians that often 20 is more accurate. This is because Russians don't understand human life—the women do not understand that they carry a person within—they do not know what gift God gave them in their womanhood. By teaching of the heart, they will come to understand the dignity of the human person. By meeting the Heart of Jesus in our prayer together, they will be healed and able to experience His love.

Unfortunately, although several women came to this meeting at first, eventually as the cold weather and dark nights of winter pressed in, they stopped coming altogether. Yet, all Sister and I had done to plan for these meetings would come to be helpful in our catechesis in other villages and cities, in Sister's teaching at the lay catechesis courses, as well as in our individual conversations and meetings with people.

A Catholic AA Group

Sister also started at this time along with a young Russian priest a very important prayer group on Wednesday nights in our apartment. It was for people with addictions (or with family members with addictions). It was based on the 12-step program, but very Catholic. In these meetings, they followed the 12-step program, yet also filled their time together with charismatic prayer with the Holy Spirit and fellowship (tea and cookies together at any meeting is very important in Russia). Confession and the different Sacraments (of Healing, of the Eucharist, of Confirmation) were also integral in the healing process for these people. They would sometimes spend their meetings discussing other spiritual topics with a Catholic flavor, such as spiritual warfare or how God delivered His people in the Exodus, and they would find concrete correlation between these things and their lives. It was almost at the beginning when Father approached and asked me to please be part of this group. There was adoration at the Claretian monastery on Wednesday nights, and I felt that Jesus wanted me to go to that—and that through that He would be helping the group meeting at our apartment. In the end, Father and Sister both said that they 'felt my prayers' those Wednesday nights and that they were very appreciative that I was in Adoration at that time. They also would both come to me to 'bounce new ideas off' me about the group (of course, they would never break confidences about what people shared there), but I would help them in general plan or brainstorm. And these meetings were anything but secret, as when I returned home our parishioners were all still there—drinking coffee and talking—and they openly spoke to me about their hearts' problems as well.

Praise, Worship and Adoration with the Young People

While this Catholic AA group met at our apartment, Jesus not only had me praying for them through resting with Him in adoration, but He also was using me in different ways at the monastery those nights. A different group of parishioners—usually youth—came for adoration at the Claretian chapel on Wednesday nights—and I would help the priests by playing a little music during adoration or in being hospitable to these guests before and after our prayer. The work that Jesus was doing in adoration on these nights was a hidden work in the hearts of the young people who would come, but it was just as powerful as the work He was obviously doing among the hearts at the 12-step meeting. Sometimes, I was very overcome by the power of the work of Jesus' Love those evenings on Dickson street, yet I never felt like I could adequately express it. I wrote home one day about this adoration saying:

> Wednesday night we had our weekly adoration at the Claretians and it was so beautiful with the priests playing guitar together while we had Russian praise and worship (a Slovakian, a Pole and an American with about 6 Russian youth). It is so amazing to me that God allows me the gift of sitting in the midst of His fire of love burning hidden away mysteriously in the taiga of Russia—the strength of the hidden prayer here touches all the world. I am so blessed to be allowed at times to see under the veil and witness the mystery of his work of the triumph of the Immaculate Heart of His Mother. And there is actual work involved. After adoration, Father and I drove four of the Russian youth home—and it took over an hour to do it. There is a lot of work just to allow four Russian youth to be

with Jesus and love Him for an hour—but that is life in the missions, I guess.[11]

Often on the drives home (when we drove the kids home), we would have beautiful conversations or times of laughing together. It was important for these kids to see, I believe, that it was important to us that they came to adoration—important enough that we would sacrifice such a long time to drive them home.

Pantomime Theater

Thursday nights we also began to have another very interesting and gifted group meet at our apartment. It was a Pantomime Theater group with some youth from our parish whose purpose was to express Gospel themes through pantomime. The particular priest who started this had studied theater a bit in Poland, attending workshops led by great pantomime masters from Germany and other places in Europe. This was his creative way of living out the Claretian charism, which was to 'preach the Gospel by every means of communication possible.' This included writing, radio, preaching, television, and also theater. This group I saw was important for many reasons. One was that many times words cannot express the deepest things in a person. Through pure pantomime (no words, no props), the Holy Spirit had the silence He needed to touch hearts powerfully—both the hearts of the

---

[11] September 21, 2001

people acting, as well as the people watching the acting. And I saw that this was very true in the case of this pantomime group in Krasnoyarsk. Also, this helped the kids in their woundedness in their bodies. I saw that almost all Russians are wounded in their bodies because of their extreme problem with child abuse as well as their lack of natural, motherly love. I noticed that in Russia mothers did not cuddle or tenderly love their children as mothers do in other places. They would hold them very distantly in their hands and not interact with them very much. I believe some of this is due to the mother's wounds from not having received tangible, pure love herself, as well as wounds in her heart from the many abortions most women had. In pantomime, these kids had to use their bodies in a beautiful way in union with the Holy Spirit—they had 'holy touch' between each other as they interacted to express Gospel Love. And this, I have to believe, healed them in some ways. Also, when people are so wounded, expressing oneself in the language of the body is easier at times than in words. And expressing oneself in the body allows for people to let go and open up, allowing Jesus' healing to enter in. The work of the Holy Spirit was very powerful within the body, mind, imagination, and emotions of those kids. And just as a person cannot touch fire without being burned, so too these kids could not be instruments in the Holy Spirit's work without being transformed from within.

I noticed that people in Russia were born and nurtured in an environment that was very anti-life. Children were seen as a burden, another problem to deal with in the midst of so many other problems. And because most women had to somehow justify in their hearts all the abortions which they underwent, they naturally were less attached to the children they actually did bear. In light of this, people generally felt very unloved in Russia. I do not know how better to put it. As I have already written, Russian children who were born into the world (as opposed to being aborted) were often abused. Such abuse, especially physical and sexual abuse, was an attack very specifically on their body. And this wound of not receiving love on a natural plane, in their five senses, made it very difficult for them to relate to God and His Love. In fact, such abuse did the opposite, it made them feel like prisoners in a body they felt was 'unlovable' or which carried deep wounds from abuse. People did not see their beauty or dignity—they were afraid to 'open' their bodies and hearts to others as they feared being wounded again, and so they did not allow God's love to enter close to heal them either. And without the powerful Love of God dwelling within them, it was very difficult for them to give themselves to others in service and love. You have to have a gift to be a gift. And these children did not see themselves as a gift, they saw themselves as a wound. In order to let God close, they first needed to feel loved by God through people and allow this tangible love to heal and free them into more supernatural Love. People in general need to feel in their bones that they are loved in order to bloom forth as the creatures of love that God created them to be.[12]

---

[12] Mary Rousseau very beautifully explains this truth in her article *Pope John Paul II's Teaching on Women*. On page 7 she writes: "But further, in order really to say a deep and heartfelt fiat to our vocation to

In light of all this, these young people who came for Pantomime Theater were actually coming to 'therapy of divine Love' without knowing it. Here they physically met Love to their bodies, as they worked together to express Jesus' Love to the parish through little skits before Mass. They had gentle, holy touch, which taught them silently of their body's dignity and holiness. And they learned to pray together with their bodies, using them as a means of transmitting the Holy Spirit to others. This was very healing to these young people whose bodies had been so unloved. And as they felt God's Love touch their bodies physically through each other, through father's instruction, and through the Holy Spirit growing and working within them, I saw them change and open up more fully to receive God close to their hearts on an interior level. I watched those kids who came at first embarrassed about their bodies and clumsy in moving them transform into confident vessels of the Holy Spirit's Love to others through their bodies

---

self-giving love, we have to believe, in our bones, in the reality of love. This basic credibility of human love is not given to us at birth, nor even at Baptism. We have to learn that love is real before we can begin to believe that it is the supremely real entity of our world; that God is Love. The conviction that love is real comes to us exactly as does our conviction of the reality of anything else-through our five senses. "How can they love God, whom they do not see," asks Saint John, "if they do not love their neighbor whom they do see?" (1 John 4:21). But before we can love, we must be loved, and know that we are loved, in some sort of sensory experience."

under the shadow of Jesus' Love which surrounded them physically, tangibly in a special way on those Thursday nights.

The Gift of Orphans

One week early that first fall in Krasnoyarsk, God gave me a beautiful gift. I was in a bookstore and I heard English. I looked up and saw a family with two small children—something odd in Russia. Because the adults were speaking English, I walked over and started talking to the babies in English. Their dad smiled and said to me, "They don't speak English yet." He explained that they were from Cincinnati, Ohio, and had just adopted these two little children the day before. Upon learning this, I spoke to the kids in Russian and they were really happy to hear something familiar. I remember their faces distinctly. Katya was 2 years old—a little petite blonde-haired girl who did not speak yet. And Dima was 3 years old, a strong stout little boy. This couple turned out to be strong Catholics and had been looking for a Church since they had arrived in Krasnoyarsk. God Himself had brought us together in this little bookstore in the middle of a city of a million people. There was a priest with us, and so right there in the store we all knelt down, and he blessed us (they were really excited for their kids to receive their first blessing.) The next day, I met them for Mass (and another couple from Florida and their newly adopted son). This adoptive mother kept in contact with sister and I for quite a while, sending pictures and updates on the children (as we continued to pray for them), and we were so happy to know that these two children were now able to grow in a happy, healthy environment coming to know God in a deep and personal way.

One thing that really struck my heart about these two children in particular was their woundedness. They had actually come from different orphanages (from different cities), yet the little boy was very concerned and loving towards the little girl—it was as if he had gotten used to caring for other children (which is not surprising since orphanages in Russia are very poorly staffed). They told me that when they ate, if something from the little girl's plate fell on the floor, he would jump down to get it for her. And at other times he would check to make sure her food was cut up well enough. He was a little father at age three. He would receive many great gifts through being adopted—a family, love, the faith, and also a chance to live his childhood (something that had evidently been denied him the first three years of his life).

I saw through our meeting with this family that the Immaculate Heart was triumphing through these little orphans as well. Our Lady said that Russia would convert the world to the love of Her Son, and I saw these little suffering children as being sent to the United States as little missionaries. I remember their mother commenting to us that she really believed in the Fatima message (which is why she wanted to adopt from Russia), and she thought that the best way for her and her husband to 'pray for the conversion of Russia' was to adopt Russia's orphaned children. They were hoping to raise these two little children in an atmosphere of Catholic, holy Love, and then send them back someday to Russia as a missionary priest and sister. I told her that we would just put that all in Jesus' sweet Hands.

The Market

Sister and I had a number of very interesting shopping experiences. I explained the complicated way of shopping in a letter I wrote home:

> After our two weeks of 'fall-rain' winter has begun to set in. It still is not freezing, but last weekend we saw the first little snow. There are many less people selling their goods on street corners. That is how we 'shop' here, you know. There are stores, but no WALMART. It's a trip for sis and I to remember what store has oatmeal, which one has sugar, which one has rice or cheese. Fruits and vegetables are usually sold on the street. Actually many things are sold on the street, from socks to shampoo to books...that's how you shop here, simply wander until you find a fork or two. Some places that 'usually' have pillows, just won't for a long time. So, our apprenticeship to life in Russia will continue as winter sets in and we need to search out where to buy items that were once on the street...I've heard some things they just don't have. You've gotta grow to like potatoes if you live in Russia in the winter 'cuz sometimes that's all you have.[13]

---

[13] October 9, 2001.

Some times, Sister's shopping adventures were spiritually fruitful, and other times that they were just plain funny. I think that the time God did not spend keeping us safe and sane while we were in Siberia that first year, He spent chuckling at us, with us, from above. Here are two stories that I found particularly cute, yet also grace-filled. The first:

Sister told me a great story that I wanted to share with you guys. It's about our anawim. Sister went to buy potatoes for us the other day (we figured we were a disgrace to Russia because we have gone so long without potatoes in our apartment.) Now Sis and I just don't eat very much, and so our potatoes often get 'eyes' on them quickly, so sis wanted to just buy 1/2 kilogram (which is about 4 or 5 potatoes). Well, I guess you don't do that in Russia. She went down to the market (a bunch of ladies standing on the street with potatoes in buckets in front of them.) She asked the first lady for 1/2 kilo and she looked at Sister like she was crazy. 'No,' she plainly said. We either had to buy the whole bucket or none. The lady standing next to this first lady looked at Sister and said, 'That lady will sell you only a few,' and she pointed to a different lady nearby. Sis walked over to her and asked for her 1/2 kilo potatoes, and this lady also looked at sis like she was crazy and said, 'No'. So, the 'friend' who had pointed this new lady out walked over to her friend and started arguing with her, trying to convince her friend to sell Sister only the few potatoes we needed. In the end, the second lady said to the third lady (her friend), 'Come on, she's a nun!!' And so, Sister received her potatoes (and offered her Mass for these nice ladies that day.) All we could think of was how Jesus said, *"And whoever gives only a cup of cold water to one of these little ones to drink because he is a disciple—Amen, I say to you, he will surely not lose his reward." Mt 10:42* They did not give water, but potatoes, only because Sister was a disciple of Jesus.[14]

And the second story:

Sister went to buy some tomatoes today, and we stopped at a little man's stand to ask how much he wanted for his little pile of vegetables. Next to him was a lady selling her produce, and she noticed Sister's habit. She asked, "Are you a missionary or something?" Sister explained that yes, she was. The lady went on to say that she was Orthodox and that she thought it was great that Sister was a missionary. She asked a few questions about America.

---

[14] June 3, 2002.

Sister, at the end of their conversation, gave the lady a holy card. Then Sister asked the man selling the tomatoes if he believed in God. He said, "Maybe I believe." Then he said something like, "I guess God puts up with a big sinner like me." Then Sister's missionary work was over because the nice lady next to him jumped into the conversation and said, "You know, we are all sinners. And plus, God does not 'put up with' anyone. He is our loving Father. God loves us all!!" It was so beautiful to hear of the Russian peddlers on the street evangelizing each other. Who would ever have thought 15 years ago that this conversation could have taken place on the streets of Russia??? O Jesus, thank you for your Mercy![15]

Sister and I would smile at our lives in joy, thanking God for allowing us to sometimes see His delicate light cut so clearly through the darkened hearts of Russia, even at the market on the streets. And I learned to focus on these little stories that showed hope instead of at the darkness ever pushing down around us.

A Mission Trip to Achinsk—Children Seeking God...

A mission trip to Achinsk during November of my first year in Siberia was full of many gifts and graces. These included spiritual encounters I had with a few little girls, a young woman who was very lost in darkness and her unborn son who became my spiritual

---

[15] August 26, 2002.

child, and a young man searching for God. The first grace had to do with two little girls I met.

One Saturday when this Sister and I went to the church to prepare for Mass, outside the gate stood a little girl bundled in winter clothes. She watched us as we entered, and wandered near us, but not to us. Sister asked me to go with her to find out what she needed. "Are you coming to us?" she asked the little girl. The little girl answered "Yes." We found out her name was Natasha and that she was 12-13 years old (yet quite little). She told us that she had heard that there would be Mass at the church, and she wanted to go. And she had never been in a church before. Now, in Russia it is not uncommon for little kids to decide on their own that they 'want God' or 'want faith' and to just wander 20-30 minutes on foot alone to go to church. Maybe their families would care less

about God, but they themselves had somewhere heard about Him and would decide that they wanted Him. The strength of these little guys amazed me. They simply decided to find Him, and they sacrificed to be with Him. This I believed was simply the result of God's powerful grace working, especially through His Mother, the true Mother of all these spiritually orphaned children. And so immediately little Natasha threw her arms around me and we were friends. Sister went ahead to prepare the altar for Mass, and I explained to my new little sister a little about the church. I asked her to look at the Stations of the Cross on the wall and tell me which one was her favorite. (I figured the Holy Spirit would guide her, and I would simply work with Him). She immediately picked out the one 'Jesus Dies on the Cross' as her favorite. So, I took her hand, and we went over to the picture. I explained about it and prayed with her about it. When we started the rosary, I taught her where the prayers were written in a little book and how to hold a rosary and how to pray. I helped her through the Mass like that as well, and that was that. The next day (Sunday) when we went for Mass in the afternoon, there stood Natasha waiting with another littler girl. As soon as I opened the car door, she yelled "Mary!" and ran up to me. She introduced me to Kristina, her little 9-year-old friend, who was pretty dirty, sick, and obviously less cared for than Natasha. Natasha said she wanted to "teach her friend about God." So, we did the whole routine over again, except this time Natasha wanted to be the teacher. She explained about genuflecting, she explained how to follow the rosary. And as we were waiting for the rosary to begin, Natasha leaned over and asked me if she could take

Kristina outside and show her the big cross. (The day before, I showed Natasha that she should kiss the big, wooden 20 ft. cross outside the church every time she came.) It was so beautiful to me to see this child's enthusiasm, hunger, love, and faith. It was always a little more work for us in church when these stray children wandered into Mass, as I had to be the one to tell them to be quiet, throw out their gum, etc., but what a joy to be allowed to mother them in their faith. God is so good.

A New Spiritual Son

Well, that same Saturday night (the day I met Natasha), I met another young girl who was about 20 years old. She was the younger sister of a

parishioner and good friend of Sister's, and Sister had asked me to please pray with her. This girl's older sister was this girl's only real support (for everyone else in their family either died or ran off). And her sister was at wits end about what to do with her. This girl had been in a lot of trouble, she was almost always constantly drunk, in trouble in her involvement with the mafia, and pregnant. This young girl herself was not a believer, but somehow I found myself at her bedside. She had been drinking, but she did allow me to come to talk with her. She even let me pray with her and over her baby within her womb. I felt immediately that she was going to have a son, and I told her that, and I asked her if I could be her son's spiritual mommy. She agreed, and I immediately consecrated him to Mary, as I knew he would have a very difficult life. I was not at all surprised when she gave birth to a boy and named him Cyril (unaware herself that St. Cyril is a powerful saint in Russia). We talked that night I visited with her about a lot of important things, none of which I really thought that she would remember or do, but I knew the love of God had to have healed her a little just in the course of our conversation. She was open to me, and He could enter a bit. She started out by crying pretty hysterically, but eventually ended in a very calm state. Her sister said she slept the whole next day. And I was happy for that—I simply prayed that Jesus would not only help and save her somehow, but also protect and nurture that poor, little baby as well soaking him in His Own merciful Love. Jesus was my only hope for them.

A Young Man on A Bus

And then Sunday night as I bused back to Krasnoyarsk, I met another interesting young man. The Holy Spirit powerfully worked with me to help him, and I myself was really surprised, yet excited by the encounter. The young man's name was Andrei. And he was 21 years old. As I had never bused between cities alone before, I was carefully watching what people were doing as I got on the bus that evening (so I understood how things worked). As I reached my seat, this kid behind me dressed in black with a black leather jacket said to me, "Hey, girl, I'm with you," meaning that his seat assignment was next to mine. His attitude was that of a young kid trying to be a 'cool man,' and I was immediately reminded of Fonzy from the TV show *Happy Days*. We sat down, and my huge

bag was on my lap as it would not fit anywhere else. I was pretty sick with a cold and I just wanted to rest alone in prayer, but I felt like God was about to do something. Still, I fought Him a little and prayed inside myself, *"I'm just going to pray for this kid. If You want us to talk, he's gotta bring it up."* Well, within 5 minutes (halfway through the second joyful mystery) this young man began our conversation. First, he just asked if I wanted him to find a place for my big bag. Then he began talking, and immediately I had to admit to him that I did not speak Russian well. The conversation moved to where I was from (America) and why I was in Russia (work for God.) I felt the Holy Spirit pushing forward within my heart the question that always gets them, and finally I just gave in and asked, "So, do you believe in God?" He answered that he used to. I remained quiet and prayed after he said this and let him come to me. I figured that my question whet his appetite. After a few minutes of silence, he told me that he was a physics student. He asked me if God was an axiom or a theorem. (A theory some people believe, or an axiom that has been proved.) I said, "Of course, he's an axiom." I gave him a few proofs for the existence of God and let him chew on them.

I also told him about Jacques Maritain and his wife's conversion. They were two very intelligent French atheist philosophers who were despairing because they could not find a real meaning in life. They agreed that if they could not find a real reason to live within a year, they would both commit suicide together. And before the year was up, God came to them through a friend, and they ended up converting and being powerful Christian

philosophers. This kid loved that story. We also talked of Léon
Bloy and a few other philosophers. And then he was quiet for a bit,
and I just rested with Jesus and tried to finish my rosary. But then
he began talking again, and he asked me if a circle could be a
square or if black could be white. "Of course not," I said. He said
that that is how he saw the spiritual life. Either he had to choose the
black path, or the white one; there was no in between. He said that
he had done some bad things, so he doubted if he even could live
on the white path anymore. And so, he had decided to just not
believe in God anymore. He knew of St. Augustine, Mary
Magdalene, and St. Paul, and so building on them I discussed with
him the great work of grace in their lives. I told him that he was
ultimately free, that belief in God was his decision. I told him that I
could (and would) pray for him and talk to him, but that in the end
it came down to what he wanted. I asked him if he wanted a life
with God or not. If he did, I told him that it would be hard, but that
his heart would find peace. If he did not, though, his heart would
never be at peace. Period. We talked about how Our Lady was the
short path to heaven. As we discussed this, a woman stood up to
exit the bus with a sleeping child in her arms, and I told him he
needed to be that child in Our Lady's arms. He needed to let Her
love carry him. He needed to trust Her Motherly love enough to
sleep in Her arms. Because only with a Mother's love can we grow,
can we rest. When we rest, we are little. We do not fight God's
work. And in this state, He is able to do miracles while we receive
in sleep, resting in His Love. I told this lost brother of mine that if
he wanted to grow in the spiritual life, he needed to let his

Heavenly Mother love him. He was amazed by what I said and by the example of the lady leaving the bus, and he stretched his neck to watch them as they went.

After that it was quiet, and then he asked me if I liked the landscape. I told him it was the most beautiful I had ever seen in the world, for I felt like I was living inside of Vivaldi's *Four Seasons*. I asked him to look out our window that was really dirty, and to tell me what he saw. And, of course, you could see the forests and countryside a little, but it was hard through the dirt. But, through the front, clean window in the bus the scenery was clear. I said that these windows were like our hearts. If they were dirty with sin, we might be able to see good and evil, the black and white path a bit, but it's hard to see and even harder to choose the good. But when our hearts were clean, the right path would be clear, and we could see our way. I told him about Confession in the Catholic Church, and that if he decides to try to know and love God and to live a life for Him, then he should really think about admitting his sins and allowing Jesus to take them, heal them (and maybe even go to Confession). He said, "Oh, it's like a clean soul. I know about that!!!" I gave him a cross I had in my pocket and asked for prayers, promising him mine. He fell asleep for the final 1-1/2 hours of our 3-hour trip, and I simply prayed for him. He thanked me when he got off a bus stop before me. And I thanked the Holy Spirit for working so powerfully in me with him, especially in my great weakness from being sick and tired.

Achinsk Retreat—Watered-Down Gas in a Blizzard

As I was eating lunch at the Claretians one day two weeks after I returned from this visit with the sisters in Achinsk, two young priests waited shyly for me after we finished eating, offering me tea and asking if they could talk with me. I loved the short time I often had with them after lunch drinking tea, and I waited for them. When they came in, one of them blurted out that he had a huge favor to ask. The two of them had to give a retreat for 20 altar boys the upcoming week in Achinsk, and they wondered if I could please come to help them out simply by my prayer. I was not too surprised that they had asked me, for I had heard two weeks before about this retreat, and Jesus immediately put on my heart that I needed to accompany them for prayer—I simply did not have the courage to tell them that. And so, I agreed in joy. One of them had to give a youth retreat to the Legion of Mary three days earlier than the altar boy retreat, and so we decided that I would just go with him to help him out on that as well—just by my prayer.

The day that we left was very crazy. Another Russian girl decided to ride with us in the car (as she would be helping out with the cooking, etc., for the Legion of Mary retreat). The Friday morning, we were to leave Father picked me up at 9:00 am to go to a village for Mass and prayers at the cemetery (for it was around the feast of All Souls), and then he said we would quickly leave afterwards. Well, plans changed. Just like a large family, car situations had to be worked out, schedules coordinated, and we did not actually end up leaving until 6:00 pm (I waited with my bags packed at the monastery all day, simply passing my time in prayer in the chapel). I felt at home while I waited, remembering our many 'car conversations' when I lived at home with my big family, conversations that were very similar to the ones we were having with the brother priests.

And so, we headed off later than planned that Friday night for Achinsk. Halfway there we stopped to get gas. It was snowing and cold, but we lived in Siberia so for us that was no big deal. Yet at about 8:00 pm that night (when it was dark) suddenly our car stopped working. It would sputter a bit whenever we went slowly and then die. When we went fast, it was fine (but the roads were icy, and so it was not the best idea to drive fast). Eventually, the car just stopped 30+ kilometers outside of Achinsk. Highways in the middle of Siberia do not have police patrol, and no one stops if they happen to pass. We could not just sit and freeze, and so Fr. and I pushed the car for about 10 minutes and then decided to try one more time, and it did turn on. But we had to go fast, or it would break again. Speeding fast in a car was very interesting in a blizzard, yet we prayed, and Jesus helped us. When we got to Achinsk and reported what had happened, everyone said, "Oh you just probably got bad gas. They probably sold you water instead of gas." Russia was the first place I had ever heard of that when you buy gas do you not know if it is water or gas.

Legion of Mary

We arrived late that night and early Saturday morning the first retreat began. It would last until Monday morning. The Legion of Mary in Krasnoyarsk was almost all kids (11-22 years old). These kids really amazed me. There was only one boy and about 10 girls. They were really unlike kids I had normally met in Russia. They seemed to be on fire for God. When I shared this thought with Father, he simply said to me, "What do you expect? They are Legion of Mary." The retreat consisted of talks given by Father on community (what is a legion), service, prayer, spiritual warfare, Mary, and the Holy Spirit. My favorite was his talk on the Joyful Mysteries of the rosary. His point was that those were places of 'difficult joy' when you think about it. The joy is hidden in them. There was suffering in each of these, but joy could be found underneath. Just as Mary found joy in the Presentation, for example, when Her Son suffered in His circumcision and she received painful prophesies, so too must we find joy in the difficult times in our life, for the will of God always has 'hidden joy.' The retreat also had group work. These kids were really creative. One day, father sent them out to evangelize the streets in groups of two, and they returned an hour later excited saying, "It really wasn't us talking, the Holy Spirit said things we never could have!!" It was beautiful to watch father make disciples of them. They all took diligent notes on what he said and put into practice his words. I watched them transform and grow. The last night we had a talent show, and the kids did everything from group crosswords to gymnastics to pantomime, to dance. Father played praise songs on the guitar and they danced and danced. One night he even took them to the cemetery to pray for the dead (because it was November). They thought that that was fun, scary, and exciting. He wanted them to be disciples of Our Lady in every respect, willing to even go to dark, scary places, even sacrificing sleep in the middle of the night to do 'crazy' things out of love for God. We also had a prayer time before the Blessed Sacrament where we all prayed over each other for the gifts of the Holy Spirit that each felt called to ask for. They asked for many things: faith, love, healing, humility, and for the gift of tongues. The person who impressed me most was little Marina, who was the youngest there. She never stopped talking and boy was she full of spiritual gifts! One would have thought that she was the oldest. She looked out for everyone. When we prayed in a group, she prayed out loud over every person asking for the gifts she felt called to pray for. What a joy this girl was, what a free, loving spirit. I really saw the fruit of all of the world's prayer for Russia in that retreat group.

An Altar-Boy Retreat

Then Monday, after the first group left, we started on our second retreat, which the two priests ran together. This was interesting. We had 20 boys, many from broken homes. And my job quickly turned from being a prayer help to being their 'mom'. Now, originally the idea they had for this retreat was for boys to discern their vocation (and he had in mind boys 13-20 years old, hoping on the older side). It ended up being many younger kids 5-14 (with maybe 3 late-teen 'helpers'). Because of the age and spiritual immaturity of the group, this retreat was real work! But Father was so open to the Holy Spirit that he went with the flow, and I saw beautiful fruits. He taught them poetry, African songs and dance, and Hebrew songs and dances. I think it was really healing for them to dance like they did in the group. I just sat in these 'conferences' and watched and prayed (my job was 'spiritual support'), and what I saw amazed me. Many of these boys had never been hugged or had been abused. They did not know what to do with their bodies, and they were a little awkward dancing. But as they would cast a glance at me every 5 minutes, and I would shake my head and tell them it was okay, good job, and to keep going, they began to be comfortable and really experienced 'boy bonding' for the first time. They clapped and marched and sang chants. They were allowed to be children, some I really believe for the first time. And this was so important to listen to the voice of God. For anyone to hear the will of God for his life, he must be a child—receptive, free in the Love of God and free in his Mother's love as well. And so, I tried to ask our Lady to be present to them in me. I watched how when I was with them and loved them, they would try things they refused when I was not there. I understood this, for on a natural level everyone needs the assurance of a mother's love when they are vulnerable or in new situations. And so, for many of these boys without a mother (or without a mother who loved them), they began to receive love through me, and I prayed that my presence would teach them of Our Lady whom they could take with them. It was a lesson for me in watching them that week—that Jesus gave us His Mother because as children we need our Mother's love to grow.

One night, the boys washed each other's hands as a sign of repentance and service. I also watched during those few days little boys with no sense of family do 'family things'. They even 'got in trouble together'. The second night they were there, a few of the kids who had also been at the bible school that previous summer with me came up and said, "Sister Mary, are we going to have that 'special prayer' with you?" I asked what they were talking about, and they said, "You know, where we have adoration and you do those special prayers over us?" And so, I asked Father about it, thinking that it was a good idea if the 12, 13, 14-year-old boys were asking for it. He agreed. And so that night we had adoration and Father, Sister T., and I prayed over them for the gifts they felt called to ask for from the Holy Spirit. I have to admit that my little Dima (about 6-years-old) was my favorite. He said that he wanted the gift of prayer so he could pray for people like we did. After we prayed over all the kids, he stayed kneeling on the priest's kneeler smack in front of the Monstrance with arms stretched out for an hour helping us 'pray' over the adults. He did not want to leave, and he remained until adoration ended at 11:00 pm, with his arms stretched out the whole time. I stayed next to him praying, and I told him a few times that if he was tired, he could sit. But he just smiled and said, "No, it's okay." Sister asked him how it felt to pray for people like that, and he answered, "It felt really, really good. So, what are we going to do now?" It was 11:00 pm after he had prayed with outstretched arms for so long, and he still was not tired. Sister told me a month later that she had a little prayer meeting with the children. And Dima prayed his heart out again with arms outstretched. He said to her, "Go ahead, Sister, pray for me again. You guys prayed for the gift of prayer and I got it. I want more gifts from God like this!!" His fire and thirst had not extinguished even over that four-week time period.

And so, a broken window, ceiling, wall, and three locked rooms later, we sent them home with a big hug. I told Father that I felt that the retreat was a great success because these kids received love, came to know who a priest was, and also learned about who a father should be through these two priests' examples. (For the priests were very fatherly these few days—they did all for them, as I was in the background and there were no sisters to tuck them in at night.) So maybe Father's originally planned discernment talks were never given, but in 10 years these little boys will remember these two young priests in cassocks who danced, sang, cleaned, and prayed with them. And if these little boys should be married someday with families, they saw in these priests for the first time what it means to be a dad. I really was amazed by their fatherly love.

Abakan

Sister from Achinsk asked me that November to please travel with her, another Sister and the priest from Achinsk, to visit the city of Abakan (which the Achinsk priests served as their parish along with Achinsk). Abakan was 400+ km south Krasnoyarsk—about a 5-hour drive. Once a month, these sisters and priest drove down there for a weekend of Masses both in Abakan as well as in the surrounding villages. They had a few people down there who were really suffering from evil spirits and needed spiritual healing. The priest had asked that I accompany them to pray with this man. I was really sick that weekend—I had not only a cold and a high fever, a severe upset stomach and diarrhea, but I also had a very bad chest cold or something that caused me to cough and have trouble breathing. Yet, as I had promised to go, I pushed through and joined them. It was a very difficult weekend for me, yet also very interesting. That Friday, we arrived in Abakan at 1:00 pm. At 2:00 pm we left for another hour drive to our first village for Mass. After that, we returned to Abakan for a second Mass there. It was already evening by the time we finished, and as I was feeling very sick the sisters went to buy me medicine, fed me all sorts of interesting 'natural remedies' such as hot beer and raspberries and hot buttermilk and honey for my cough, and put me to bed early. Saturday morning, we had to wake up early to drive another 150km (1-½ hours) to another village just to hear Mass for two 80-year-old babushkas. They only knew the Mass in German, so we prayed in Russian, and they responded and sang in German. I was surprised yet happy that we had driven all that way just to pray Mass with these two little babushkas. After Mass, we cleared the table we had turned into an altar and set it for a quick lunch. Afterward, we drove another hour out to another village where we prayed Mass in another house. And then we drove another 1 1/2 hours home. Sunday, we had Mass in Abakan and then headed back to Krasnoyarsk.

It was after Mass on Sunday that we prayed with the couple of people who needed healing. We took them individually into a little room off to the side. I talked for a long time with one man, who actually knew English. He was originally from China, had suffered a horrible life, including having to live with a step-mom or aunt (I do not remember) who had used black magic in front of him and on him. He suffered from this and needed lots of prayers to help in his spiritual warfare.

A Night on the Trans-Siberian Railroad

A priest once asked me to go with him that fall to Achinsk for two days as he had to give a day of recollection for the two sisters there—and he wanted me to come and help him in prayer and simple guidance. I was just like a spiritual mama. So, we left on a Monday night on the 8:00 pm train. Father was a little tired and thought that he would have a nice, quiet conversation with me (and maybe work a little on his talks for the next day), but I ruined his plans with my missionary fire. I later wrote home about this experience:

The trains at night were not always a pretty sight in Russia, especially in the cheapest sections (which meant that the compartments were open, and seats were first come, first serve.) Many times at night on the trains people were all just drunk. Well, this was partially our experience that Monday night. But sitting across from us was a young couple and a little boy, three-years-old, with two big patches on his face. And I knew that I had to give him (the little boy) a holy card of Jesus. So, I rummaged through my bag while Father (who knows me by now) asked what I was up to now. When I told him, he said, "Mary, THAT little boy? He's so little, he won't understand." But I felt like I needed to and so I just said, "Sure he will, Father. Watch. Obedience to the Holy Spirit is obedience to the Holy Spirit. I don't have a choice." He smiled wryly at me and watched.

The little boy started talking to me right away, only half interested in the picture. He wanted to tell me all about his bandages and I came to understand that they had been in a pretty bad car accident in Krasnoyarsk. Over and over again he told me (and showed me with his hands) how the car swirled and flipped and how he had to go the hospital and how he cried. Many times he said, "It went bang! And I was at the hospital and I cried." He was so adorable!! (He reminded me of my nephew Michael Jeffery who was his age and had a similar personality. He talked and talked. He was very intelligent and used big words. He was really polite and full of lots and lots of energy.) As I missed my little nephews and nieces at home, being with him I thought I was in heaven!! As he talked with me his parents chimed in with quiet, little explanations to help Father and I understand his story. They were from Achinsk, their car was totaled, and they had no way back from

Krasnoyarsk but the train. Father was watching, amazed that the old picture of Jesus worked in that a conversation was born with these strangers. Father himself started getting excited and said, "Mary, where are your Miraculous Medals, give the parents them." (As I always carried Miraculous Medals on me so that I could give them to people.) I pulled a few out, and gave them to him saying, "You go ahead, Father, you've gotta explain what they are, and your Russian is way better than mine, obviously (as he was Russian.)" And so, he did. The dad said, "I wish we had these yesterday before the crash." And I said, "Yeah, I understand, but see Mary allowed that so that we could meet on this train, have this conversation, and you could receive Her medal...see how She loves you??" They actually agreed with me. Then the Mom looked at me and asked, "So are you guys Mormon?" (Unfortunately, there were a lot of Mormon missionaries in Russia, and people were afraid of them. And so, when a person heard the word missionary, they often would think, "Oh no, a Mormon!") I replied to the mom, "No, we're Catholic." And she asked, "So what is the difference between Catholics and Orthodox anyway?" I felt like the Holy Spirit was calling for me to hand this question off to my wonderful Russian priest counterpart. I said, "I could answer your question, but he could much better answer because of his language...Father, would you explain to them?" Father was glowing. And so, from these first minutes on the train for the next 4 HOURS they drilled Father with questions about the Church, Jesus, and Faith in general. The lady was especially a

tough cookie, asking good and difficult questions, but Father answered everyone. We watched her soften in the course of our conversation (as Father had a gentle charm as well as great love as he explained the often confused truth about God, Faith, and the Church.) By the end of their conversation, she said that they had seen the Catholic Church in Achinsk and that maybe they would even visit. The whole time Father was speaking to this couple I acted as the babysitter for little Daniel who decided to fall in love with me and asked me if he could be 'MY little boy'— this is translated like if I would be his girlfriend.

And so while his mom and dad were talking to Father, I was trying to calm down this little boy who was awfully excited about having a new friend. He was trying to run up and down the aisle and to climb up on things. I tried desperately to keep him still with me, as I was a little afraid of the drunken people on the train hurting him. One compartment over from us was another family and another little boy—Viteer. I was worried about little Daniel running into this little boy's family, which consisted of three or four adults who were all really drunk (so drunk that they could not walk.) And little Viteer (who was about five) was just sitting there, staring at me. I sort of played hide and seek with him a little from afar while I was also playing with Daniel, but I did not dare go up to him because I knew that his already screamy, drunk parents would just make a scene. Yet the Holy Spirit took over in Daniel so that a little of Jesus' Love could be shared with Viteer as well. All of the sudden, after Daniel had become acquainted with my rosary, learned that it was not a toy (although he proceeded to use Jesus as a sling shot), and actually become the owner of it, he turned to me and said, "I want to share this rosary with that little boy." Mind you, Daniel had NEVER heard about Jesus until our conversation, and suddenly he, at three years of age, wanted to be a missionary. I said, "Go ahead." Daniel called the little boy over and asked, "What's your name?" And after they exchanged names he said, "Look, this is Jesus, and He is not a toy." And together they stared at the crucifix for a minute. Then Viteer came up to me and said, "I know Jesus Christ and I know He is not a toy, can I have a rosary, too?" So, I found my backup rosary and handed that off as well. And through their common rosaries, a friendship was born between these two little boys. For a while they played a Russian version of 'tag,' where Daniel was the fish and Viteer the fisherman. When later Daniel was getting tired and started to whimper on my lap, Viteer came up to him and said, "Don't cry little fishy, it will be alright." What love in this heart of a child from such a family!! Jesus truly loved this little boy. As they grew tired, I was very glad that I had brought along my Russian copy of *The Little Prince* and we looked at the pictures. In the end, I taught them a few prayers (like, *"Jesus I love you. Jesus, help me be a good boy"*), and Viteer promised to pray for me too. Daniel asked a jillion times (like only a 3-year-old would) if I would please be a guest at their house someday.

And so, as Father, the Russian (who is brilliant, knows the Church, speaks like 7 languages, etc.) catechized the adults, Jesus worked a little miracle through the little ones and allowed me to watch it. I was so happy for that privilege. And I thought that if the Holy Spirit could work so strongly through a 3- and 5-year-old in the middle of frozen Russia (frozen not only physically, but also spiritually), then I had to be sure that He also was working powerfully in my life and in the lives of all those I loved and prayed for. In this encounter on the train that bland Monday night, I saw the little flicker of God's Presence in the Russian's hearts, and I caught a glimpse of His work for the Triumph of Mary's Heart not only in what was still a pretty communist Russia, but also in the entire world.

Graces of God on a Winter's Day

God often was present to me during these years in Siberia in simple, everyday encounters I had with people. I saw His hand of Love work in hidden ways, and when I witnessed such occurrences, I would be filled with great joy and hope. I remember one evening how I had one of those miraculous walks home from Church were I was simply amazed at God's Hand. About 15 minutes from the Claretians, I saw a lady begging. She was literally frozen. I could not see her face because she was wrapped up in clothes, so I was not sure if I knew her from the previous summer or not (when I had spent a little time doing ministry with the beggars). Well, I stopped and dug into my pocket where I found a few coins and a

miraculous medal. As I reached down (she was sitting on the curb) to place the coins in her plastic cup, she looked up at me saying, "Thank you." She could not tell who I was either because only my glasses were showing, as everything else was wrapped up in scarves, 3 hats, and my coat. Then this woman saw the miraculous medal in my hand as I said, "This is the Blessed Mother, She is your Spiritual Mother and She loves you." She interrupted me at the end of my sentence and exclaimed, "Oh Mary!! Thank you!! May God bless you." She knew me from the medal. I was taken back that she remembered my name as Mary (not the Russian Masha or Maria or some other variation that people just start calling me). She remembered me, was filled with joy from the medal, and gave me her blessing. This just really touched me on that dark, frozen night. And so, I went around the corner, and saw another lady whom I could not recognize. I dug into my pockets again and pulled out a few more coins and a St. Benedict medal. I slowed down deliberating whether or not to give the medal with the money because saints were really hard to explain to unbelievers and also because so often people there mixed-up holy medals or rosaries with pendants or luck charms. In the end, I decided to be careful and just give her the money in love, offering a prayer with it. I reached down into her plastic container, and then I looked up straightening up from bending down, I literally almost run into an old man with a cane, who asked me, "Could you please sacrifice something for me??" as he put out his cup. I had given my last kopek to the lady before him, and so all I had left in my hand was the St. Benedict medal I had decided not to give her. "I don't have anything else," I said. "All I have is this." And he looked down into my hand. I said, "All I have is this St. Benedict medal..." And as I said 'Saint' he said, "Please give me that, please give me that!" And so, I did. I said that St. Benedict would help him, especially in his battle with the devil. And I asked him to pray for me. I left him as he said, "Lord, bless her, bless her." And so, I finished my walk overwhelmed at the swift, gentle, warm breeze of the Holy Spirit that had just brushed over me in a matter of 3 minutes. In those three minutes I really had felt the hand of God touch me as He called me to love His littlest sheep I met on the streets. I believe that I received more that evening then those three people, for I received a big fire in my heart as God's fiery Love passed through me to reach those beggars. Once again, I rejoiced in how good God was.

Babushkas

The faith of some of the Russians is amazing, especially the faith of the Russian babushkas.[16] Often

---

[16] Babushka means 'grandmother' in Russian, and a person calls any older woman 'babushka' or 'baba'.

times it was the babushkas who kept the faith alive during the many years of Communism's dark reign. I met many babushkas in my stay in Russia, and they each had their own very interesting story. Baba Masha was one example of this. I remember one day when she came over to the Claretian monastery for lunch with us. Bless her heart, right in the middle of our conversation about how a good Russian eats lots of bread with every meal and why I did not eat more bread, she broke down into tears about her life. This lady was a strong woman. She prayed all day, but I also remember her coming over to drink a shot or two of vodka with one of the priest's mothers on her birthday. She had worked supporting her family for many years in the coal mines. And now as an older lady, she devoted her entire day to prayer. She would wake up every morning at 5 or 6 o'clock AM to say her rosaries, then she would clean a little, then pray some more rosaries, then she would start in on lunch, and then say some more rosaries. After that she would nap, take a bath to get ready for bed (the 40-minute walk to Mass and 40-minute walk home is a little too much for her some days, so although sometimes she would go during the week, usually she only attended on Sunday), and then she would pray before bed. Her life was like a good hermit's. Anyway, this afternoon she broke down into tears, saying how she loved God, tried to be faithful, only prayed all day, and did not understand why she suffered so much. She asked why so many bad things happened. Then she interrupted herself saying, "I mean I'm not questioning God or anything, He's in charge, and of course He is only Love and He always gives what is best for me....I just don't understand." Her life had been very hard, but her faith was amazing.

I had one other 'favorite babushka'. She was Sister's and my new babushka at church in the springtime that first year in Krasnoyarsk. The week before Easter Sister, and I were sitting at church before Mass when a new babushka came in and sat down beside us. She began to speak in a very loud voice, and as Sister tried to quietly answer her questions, she explained again loudly that she could not hear. This was our linguistic challenge number one. My dear Sister tried to help out and write her a message on paper, when we in turn found out that she could not read either (she was almost blind.) This was our linguistic challenge number two. To complicate matters, she was orthodox, and did not understand why she could not go to Communion. She told us that starting that day she really wanted to be Catholic. Confession was difficult for her because she was deaf and would scream her sins and could not hear the answers that the priest spoke to her. She had come to our church because she said she was troubled with bad spirits, and someone told her that only the Catholics could help her. Somehow the Lord worked, pitying her childlike heart and faith, and within a few days of her arrival in our pew she got to Confession and began to receive Jesus. The priest said that although he explained the differences in Orthodox and Catholic faith to her, she was so simple she could not understand and just cried because she wanted to receive Jesus in the Eucharist. He made a pastoral decision and simply allowed her to, realizing that she would never understand the difference in her mind—to her there was one Jesus, and she wanted to receive Him. Her faith and heart were very simple and beautiful. The first week she began coming, she stared at Sister and I the whole Mass, and if we folded our hands under our chin, so did she; if I prayed with my head down on my lap, so did she. She copied everything perfectly because she "wanted to be Catholic" and wanted to do things just like we Catholics did. She was greatly relieved when we assured her it was okay, she made the sign of the cross differently (she kept forgetting how we did it).[17] Every day she would come to church before us and set songbooks on the seats next to her saving them for us. If we arrived before her and sat in a different seat (the same row and place, but maybe one seat over), she would become upset and make us move when she got there. She wanted to sit in the exact same place every day. She would bring us pickles, tea, and all sorts of goodies. And she was really full of joy!! At the end of Mass every day she would ask, "Can I put on my coat now and go home?" She was one of my greatest simple joys every day. I praised God that our dear Orthodox babushka found a home in the Catholic Church.

Lent and Easter, 2002

The Russian word for 'Lent' means 'the Great Fast,' and I quickly understood that year the reason for this meaning. Russians took Lent very seriously, much more seriously than most

---

[17] Catholics make the Sign of the Cross one way, and the Orthodox make it a different way.

Americans I know. Growing up we were taught that we should give 'something' up for Lent—either sweets, pop, T.V., etc. When I was in high school, I heard for the first time that it was good for a person to not only make a sacrifice during Lent (such as 'giving something up), but it was also important to try to pray more (I came to understand which is why we always said the family rosary together during Lent) as well as to help the poor. Yet those Russians who recognized Lent as a holy season of the year (which often included people who never had stepped in a church) fasted as I had never seen before. It was assumed among our parishioners and the babushkas we visited in the country that a person would never eat anything sweet all Lent; many also assumed that a person would never touch meat all of Lent. Some people went so far as to restrict their diets to three or four foods in general. I was glad that I had picked up on this early on because I could have really scandalized someone. Although growing up I always gave up sweets, coffee, or other difficult things during Lent, the way I approached Lent had changed the deeper my spiritual life grew. Giving up sweets, for example, was no longer a big sacrifice as it had been years before. And so, for Lent I tried to fast on bread and water more often, but when I was not fasting, I never would have thought twice about eating sweets—for I had not given that up. Yet the first parish pantomime theater gathering we had during Lent I learned my lesson, for I always made some sort of sweet for the kids to eat during break or after everything had ended. Yet Fr. L. (as well as the kids) were surprised that I had prepared something sweet during Lent, and they decided that I should not do that again until Easter. They said that we could provide rolls for the kids or something simple like that—but not sweets. It was a beautiful sacrifice that they wanted to make as a parish group together, and so Sister and I would make sure that we had plenty of bread rolls and butter waiting for them after their meeting.

Stations of the Cross with the Youth

Early on in Lent during one of our trips to Kansk Father decided that he wanted our youth group meeting on Sunday afternoon to be focused on the theme of the Stations of the Cross. One of the sisters really wanted to help out with this meeting, so I stepped back (as Father and I usually planned the meetings) and Father allowed her to plan it—his only stipulation was that he really wanted for the kids to live the Stations in some way. He said that he did not want an ordinary meeting where our teenagers simply listened to someone speak about Jesus' sufferings or where they simply prayed the Stations by reading pretty meditations. He asked the sister to please try to think of a way to help our teenagers really take Jesus' sufferings to their hearts. Well, Sister planned a nice meeting consisting of a short talk, each kid drawing a Station in silent meditation and then group prayer. Father left Sister alone to try to implement her plan, and he simply prayed that Jesus would somehow touch the kids' hearts (even if the meeting seemed a little boring). And the Holy Spirit paid great attention to the desires of Father's heart—that the kids really feel something of

Jesus' sufferings on the Cross—and He arranged that Sister's plans were altered a bit by providence in a very unpredictable way.

Many of the kids who came that Sunday had never even heard of such a thing as the Way of the Cross or even much about Jesus' suffering and death in general. And so, we knew that regardless of what was planned, it would be an eye-opening, grace-filled afternoon for many of their hearts. The first thing we did when the kids arrived at our apartment was to feed them. Because everything in Russia was really expensive, the kids just did not usually eat right. They would always arrive hungry, and so Sister usually made a simple Ramon-Noodle-Like Soup thing, and we also gave them bread, fruit, and milk (these were things hard for them to come by normally). Well, that particular Sunday, as lunch was about to begin, there was a knock at the door, and I went to answer it. Two young people (a guy and a girl) stood there, and I smiled and let them in although I did not recognize them. Often, we would get new people at our meetings, and Sis and I had prayed hard that Our Lady would bring who SHE wanted this particular Sunday, and so I did not think twice about letting these two young people in. Yet about 30 seconds after I let them in, I realized that they were really drunk. (Saturday, the day before, had been the Russian holiday for Russian men, and so these young people had been out partying all night.) The guy was a Pentecostal, and he immediately started to drill me with many questions about the Catholic faith. Father came up behind me pretty quickly, so I handed our two new guests off to him to deal with.

This priest was very loving with them, and he invited them in with his gentle kindness and proceeded to answer all of their questions, showing them places in the Bible to support his answers. I was impressed at his choice to take these kids seriously (seeing they were really drunk). After a good hour, he and Sister began the normal youth group session, and I took the girl (they had not wanted to leave, yet also did not want to participate fully in the general meeting), and I convinced her to eat and drink some coffee. I figured that Our Lady brought them there for a reason, and if I could help her sober up a little, then maybe we could talk. She took what I gave her, and it worked. I had a nice little conversation with the girl (who was a cousin or sister of one of our normal youth group members), who was living with this boy although they were not married (and who also had given birth to their child). Our afternoon was spent in trying to keep our two drunken guests from disturbing our other kids from their meditation on the Cross. Yet, in the end, the guy began to really scream and yell and so we had to ask them to leave. Many of the kids were upset by the whole incident, but I was simply amazed how God answered Father's prayer. He wanted the kids to experience the Way of the Cross, and Jesus knew that nice songs and silent prayer would not teach the lesson of Love and the ugliness of the Cross that this incident did. The kids also were forced to live mercy. We explained all this to the kids, and they were open in trying to understand it. All in all, I considered the afternoon a success, for our kids had witnessed real Love crucified. Regardless of their rudeness and sin, we had welcomed and loved this couple and tried to truly answer their questions and help their lives. Even asking them to leave was a witness of Love, for we did it in gentleness—not in an obnoxious way—and we held no grudge against them. And our teenagers had felt what the Cross was like as they listened to screaming and mocking voices in the room next door as they sat in our chapel trying to focus on the Cross and pray. That is what the Cross really had been similar to—for Jesus was crucified not in a quiet, pretty chapel, but instead in the midst of a loud city with drunk people yelling and mocking Him. Even though it seemed to poor sister at first that she had failed miserably, I tried to help her see the great hidden beauty in all that had occurred. In the end, I think she could see the mysterious Hand of God working in it all. Yet we were glad, nonetheless, that a similar situation never occurred again.

I was also amazed upon reflecting on it all later how God had used the sin of these kids to help their souls. God had not wanted them drunk, but He took advantage of their weak state of mind to get them to come to a place where they could meet Him, a place they never would have come sober. The girl and I had a long talk, and if nothing else in the end she wanted to grow in her Catholic faith and to give it to her unbaptized daughter. She even had joined in the prayer that afternoon for a little bit. We could have turned these two lost souls away as soon as we saw that they were drunk, but I was glad that the Spirit had guided us otherwise. I thought afterwards how maybe this was the only chance they would ever have in their lives to receive Love or to know God. We had to just pray that His Spirit was stronger than the darkness of their lives and able to enter their hearts and somehow change them even in the midst of their drunkenness. I also was reminded as we were sitting at the table, drawing pictures of Jesus on the Cross (I was doing this with the guy trying to keep him from screaming so that the rest of the kids could meditate in silence), of what the Pope had told us in his encyclical on the New Millennium where he asked us to 'go out into the deep.' If these kids were not in the deep, dark waters, if they were not the ones all would think hopeless cases to save, I do not know who is. And I also was reminded of the Charism of SOLT, which is to serve those no one else wanted to. Who would want to give Jesus to a bunch of drunk teenagers? But they needed Him. And through the grace of our charism, we were allowed to serve Jesus in this way. In the end, I simply saw in them the same plight I see in all the world, even in my own heart. I saw in them the truth that I also must embrace: the truth that we need God, we need a Savior.

There were many other neat graces of that first Lent in Siberia. Palm Sunday in Krasnoyarsk was especially blessed for me. After Mass that Sunday morning, we had a beautiful play put on by the children and teenagers of the parish. They had practiced so long and hard at our apartment for it, and in the end they really pulled off a professional-looking passion play. The Friday before Palm Sunday they had performed a Pantomime Stations of the Cross, and this Sunday they had a normal play with music and all. It was really beautiful how Father and Sister had interwoven the story of Adam and Eve and the Fall of Man within the story of Jesus' Redemption of mankind. The opening scene of our play was in

Eden, and at the end of it, little Eve (who had been torn away from Adam in Satan's temptation) turned into Mary, the New Eve, at the foot of the Cross. It was truly amazing and deep, bringing me to tears.

Holy Week in Achinsk and Kansk

The Sunday, Monday, Tuesday, and Wednesday of Holy Week I spent with the two young priests in Achinsk helping with another retreat for the altar boys. It ended up that we had about 20 boys, ranging in ages of 6 to about 16. The priests decided that the little guys would be bored training in the Church for long periods of time, and so I got assigned on the spot to the little boys. We had our own little retreat, reading stories about Holy Thursday, Good Friday and Easter, drawing, and even putting together a few little plays that we performed for the older boys. I really loved these little boys (this was not the first time I ended up getting them assigned to me on retreats), and we had a special bond for on retreats they knew that they were 'always with Mary.' When they did not want to do what we needed to, I often bribed them with chocolate, and so they quickly grew to love me for that especially.

While I had been with the two priests in Achinsk, Sister had headed off to Irkutsk with the other priests for the chrism Mass, which was held on Tuesday of Holy Week. The plan was that one priest and I would travel from Achinsk to Kansk and meet up with Sister and another priest (who was the present official pastor of the parish in Kansk) who would travel to Kansk from Irkutsk. The four of us would spend Holy Thursday-Easter Sunday serving together in Kansk. That Easter Triduum was very grace-filled that year. I do not think I had ever before experienced the Triduum and Easter so spiritually intensely. Naturally, the Church in Russia takes these days very seriously. In America, we would always go to church on these days (and spend Good Friday between noon and 3:00 pm in prayer), but I had never taken them as a special time of retreat as we were to do. And our hearts benefited deeply from this. Holy Thursday was considered a big feast day—a day celebrating in great joy the feast of Our Lord's first Mass. Yet after Mass on Thursday evening until Saturday night's vigil Mass, everyone was encouraged to strictly fast (either not eating at all or only eating bread). Yet after Mass Saturday night, as well as Sunday morning after Mass, we had great feasts. The people all brought their food for feasting to Mass on Saturday night for the priest to bless. The Russians made special breads and eggs just for the Easter feast. They also brought their meat, butter, and salt—really a sample of everything they would eat—to be blessed.

Father had decided that the four of us would spend our Easter Triduum as special days of recollection (in the time we were not serving the parish), and so he assigned each of us different times every day to give reflection talks. It was a beautiful time of silence and adoration with Jesus in our little apartment in Kansk as we prepared for His Resurrection!! Saturday, one of the priests taught me how to decorate eggs 'Polish style,' by dying them using onionskins and then carving them with a needle. It was truly a joyous time. And I really loved how we ended our Easter Sunday morning Mass by Adoration for a bit.

The best thing about Easter in Siberia was how people rejoiced in the Resurrection. They really rejoiced! The normal Catholic greeting of "Praise be Jesus and Mary—Now and Forever" was changed to "Christ has Risen—Truly He has Risen!" Everyone rejoiced to walk around and simply say that to everyone. In this, I truly felt Jesus' presence of hope.

Retreats in Kansk week after Easter—Teaching the Vocation of the Holiness of Womanhood

The week after Easter Sister left for Rome to renew her visa. She would be gone for three weeks. The situation in Russia was pretty rough for missionaries. Not only was the Bishop still forbidden to return to his diocese, but protests against Catholics began to spring up throughout the country. One weekend, 4000 Orthodox gathered in Krasnoyarsk for anti-Catholic rallies. Similar gatherings took place throughout 20-30 cities throughout Russia. Because of all the anti-Catholic hatred filling the air, we missionaries were advised to be a little more careful and to stick together.

One priest and I were planning at this time to go to Kansk for a week. He was going to give a retreat for the altar boys there at a resort nearby, and I was planning to give a retreat for the girls in the parish apartment on the theme of what it meant to be a woman of God. Considering the anti-Catholic atmosphere throughout Russia, Father's superior suggested that we try to find another priest or young man from the parish to travel with us (for two men would be better protection than one). Although Father asked all his priest brothers, the altar boys, and other active parishioners if they would like to join us, a week was too long for any of them to be away from Krasnoyarsk, and so we ended up having to go alone. We could not even convince some of the young ladies who helped with the Legion of Mary or Pantomime groups to come with us. A week was just too long of a time. Yet in looking back I see how Jesus Himself arranged this situation for us so that He could teach us many lessons He otherwise would not have been able to.

Once we got to Kansk, our plan was for Father to take the boys away for their retreat (although they would return every day to eat lunch with us), while I would stay at the apartment alone and the girls would simply come in the morning and return home at night. This was not ideal, since it was a bit dangerous for me to be staying alone in that apartment, yet we had no choice. And so, Father and I decided to simply trust Jesus.

I tried to split the retreat with the young women into several parts: prayer, reflections, journaling, sharing, and songs. I also had a few fun things planned for us. One day, for example, I prepared pretty, little cards with women's saints' names written on them (with their picture). Each of the girls picked one to be their special saint and role model. And I had saint books readily available so that they could look up the life of their saint and write down the interesting facts they wanted to remember. The retreat consisted of 5 basic talks on the theme of "The Dignity of Womanhood." The first was about how women were created to be a gift and a helpmate. The second was about how women were created to receive and protect life, and to be mothers. The third had to do with vocations. The fourth was about purity. And the fifth was about the relationship of women with the Cross and with the Eucharist. Father asked me to tape the talks that I gave for him. I had planned these talks a little bit, basing them on Scripture. Yet more than anything, the Holy Spirit guided me profoundly as I began to speak—giving me concrete examples and analogies, which the girls could relate well to. All in all, I think that the retreat was very successful in that each of the girls left knowing a little deeper the great beauty, gifts, worth and possibility with which God had created them.

A Brush with Death and A Lesson of Trust

This week in Kansk was not only a week of growth for our young parishioners, yet also a week when Jesus taught my (and Father's) hearts deep lessons of trust and His Love. One such lesson occurred one of the nights I was alone in the apartment. It was May 2nd, the day after the huge communist work holiday. And the whole city had been out drinking and celebrating all day, all night, and all day again. Around 9:00 pm that evening as I was in my little room working on the computer, three men came to my door. Now I had been instructed very seriously to not answer or open the door to anyone while I was alone in the apartment. And so, I figured that whoever it was would simply leave. Yet then I began to hear male voices talking. They grew louder, and the men started screaming through the door at me to open up. I did not know if they knew who I was or that I was in the apartment alone—or if maybe they simply knew that Catholics lived there. Regardless, I did not want to yell back, for if they did not know that I was a foreign girl, it would be obvious from my voice and accent. And that fact would give even more fuel and fire to their drunken desire to come through the door. The men began screaming louder and louder, beating on the door. At this, I became quite afraid. I did not have the phone number of the police or parishioners whom I could call for help. I did not even know our address or phone number in the apartment. As the door shook from their pounding and I feared they would break through, I looked for a place to hide—yet I did not fit under the bed and there simply was nowhere else to go. The apartment was on the 5th floor, and so I could not jump out the window. Even if I had wanted to risk the high jump, below me was a 20-foot-deep hole full of bare pipes and sewage where the city was 'doing construction.' I began to panic. I began to shake and cry. I wanted so bad to trust Jesus, yet I was petrified. I did not feel the grace I needed to be a martyr. I felt like I was not ready to be raped and killed. I told Jesus that if He was trying to teach me something, to please not teach me through such fear. I agreed to do anything He wanted, but I begged Him to please simply teach me and guide me in Love rather than in the fear I felt consume me. Oh, I begged and begged. Finally, I remembered seeing a phone directory for the diocese in one of the rooms. At this point the men had been pounding for 7 or 8 minutes. No one in the building would come out to help me, for Russians learned during the time of Communism when neighbors were secretly arrested at night for no reason at all that they simply needed to 'look the other way' so as to avoid problems themselves. I found the phone directory, yet I did not know how to call long distance. I tried many combinations of numbers and finally was able to call the priests in Krasnoyarsk. One of the priests answered the phone and I immediately began crying in a whispering voice to him. I said, "Father, they are going to kill me. These men are here, beating on the door, and they are going to come in, rape me and kill me. I want to trust Jesus, but I just can't calm down. I'm just not ready to die. Please help me." Now, this priest was 250 km away from me, and so he felt helpless. He gave the phone to someone else to talk with me and he ran to find out the address of the Kansk apartment for me. After that he called the police in Krasnoyarsk who called the police in Kansk. After about 15 or 20 minutes of pounding and screaming, the men left. And eventually the police came, as well as some parishioners who we finally got a hold of. I felt guilty that I had not been calmer—I had truly wanted to trust Jesus with all my heart. I wanted to surrender in fiat even to death. My body, mind, and emotions had simply not cooperated with my heart. I shook for hours after everyone left that night. Yet in that all Jesus did teach me something beautiful about trust; and in that situation He prepared and formed me so that when I was in other situations where I could have feared similarly, He was able to gather my emotions, mind, and body and help teach me to truly fiat with all I was.

Another Retreat with Young Girls— Seeking the Lost Sheep

I returned home the summer of 2002 to visit my family and renew my visa. As soon as I got back to Russia on July 30th, Sister and I only had a few days to catch up and make some important decisions before I left again for Achinsk. There was a Sister (my Russian spiritual daughter) who was planning to leave on August 19th for Poland to study for a year, and she had asked that I please come to visit her for two or three days before she left. Yet, when I arrived, she and some of the other sisters in her order were just about to start a two-week long retreat for a group of girls (15-25ish), and the priest in charge asked me to please stay to be prayer help for them. I strongly felt that my 'work' in Russia this second

year would not be as active as the previous one—but instead more of simply a work of me being a presence of prayer. I prayed about whether or not I should stay, and I felt Jesus tell me that I could, as long as I live the vocation, He was calling me to while I was there.

We had a very interesting combination of girls on this retreat—girls from our Legion of Mary group in Krasnoyarsk to girls who had never before stepped in a church. And each of them had her own story. One girl that really touched me was Rita. Rita just happened to be passing through Achinsk on the Sunday before the retreat started on Monday. She had school exams to take in town and was staying with her aunt, who invited her to Sunday Mass. Rita had never been baptized, and had never actually been in a Church before, and when her aunt invited her with her to Mass she simply thought, 'Sure, why not.' Well, at Mass that Sunday Rita met Sister (who was friends with her aunt) and who invited her on this retreat with us. In the end, Rita agreed to go take her exams on Monday, and then remain in Achinsk an extra two weeks to take part in the retreat. This girl had an amazingly simple and open heart and took everything in very deeply. By the third or fourth day, her heart was already aching for Baptism. She believed in the true Presence and although she could not go to Confession, she asked to at least go and 'talk with the priest' while we had Confessions. If she had been two years younger (she was around 16), Father said that he would have baptized her at the end of our retreat. But because anyone over 14 years of age is considered an adult in the Church, she was too old to simply baptize without the Bishop's permission (unless it was an emergency). She was planning to stay and study in Achinsk the following year, and we were hoping that she would continue to come to Church for catechesis and be able to receive Baptism within a few months.

Another interesting girl that God's Providence brought to our retreat was Maria. Her mom came to the Church a week before the retreat and told the sisters that she wanted to give her 15-year-old daughter to the convent. As the sisters talked with her and asked her why, she responded that she knew that religious sisters did not do anything, and her 15-year-old did not want to do anything (she simply ran away all the time) and so her mother thought she would make a nice nun and wanted to give her away. This woman said that she herself was Orthodox, but that she did not want to give her daughter to the Orthodox convent because she saw on TV that although Orthodox sisters do absolutely nothing, Catholic sisters ride bikes and play with balls and she thought that her daughter could do that. When I first heard this story from the sisters, I thought they were joking, but once I met Maria and her mother myself, I realized the sad reality of it all. Well, God truly blessed the sisters in Achinsk with a special grace to help this family, and even after that funny explanation of everything, they still took the time to speak with this woman and her daughter for quite some time. They came to find out that this woman was actually searching for God and the truth, and that she did have a serious problem with her 15-year-old running away all the time. The family had many problems and in the end we realized that this poor girl just really needed love. Father agreed that if Maria wanted to come and see the retreat for a day, and wanted to stay with us, she could. Well, she did come. And she did stay. Her clothes were really immodest and so the sisters told her she needed new clothes in order to stay. They told her mom to buy her a pair of jeans and a few t-shirts so that she looked like a little girl (and not a woman of the streets). Maria excitingly agreed and ran around the group of her new friends asking if she could take their clothes to show her mom what to buy. By the third day, she herself was saying that she wanted to be a sister, although I think she just had never seen so much love in one place in her life. Maria fell sick a few days into the retreat and had to return home, but we trust that God's great mercy was guiding all. Her mother continued to come to Mass almost every day after her first meeting with the sisters, and she wanted to be brought into the Catholic Church.

On the same trip to visit this sister I also spent time with some Russian ladies (blood sisters) who also were suffering from similar deep childhood wounds. I did not know how to love them except by doing little things like getting them a glass of water in love and being a cup receiving Jesus' Presence of Love in their midst. Such situations were extremely difficult for me, yet they strengthened me in my vocation in many ways. I saw that hearts that were so deeply wounded could not be helped except by the grace and touch of Jesus' Powerful Love. And so, my words or actions could not help them as much as my suffering life in fiat love with Jesus on the Cross. In that, His Love would somehow be made visible to them.

Chapter 5

You Simply Must Love Her

"Above all, let your love for one another be intense, because love covers a multitude of sins..."
(1 Peter 4:8)
"It bears all things, believes all things, hopes all things, endures all things. Love never fails."
(1 Cor 13:7-8)

-

Love is the most powerful weapon against evil. It is the instrument which can most profoundly, quickly, and gently transform a person. It is often the only tool a missionary can always access as a help to serve those entrusted to him. Love resembles fire in three ways. First, just as everything that is thrown into fire is turned into fire, everything thrown at a heart that loves is consumed by Love and turned into Love. The greatest weakness, sins, sufferings, and brokenness can be transformed into great weapons of salvific, sacrificial Love when a heart simply accepts them and unites them to Jesus' sacrifice on the Cross (where He took all of humanity's sins, weaknesses, sufferings, and brokenness onto Himself). When the most difficult or darkest of situations encounters Love, it is immediately transformed. And when the most difficult people encounter Love, they too are immediately transformed. Love touches people and changes them. Secondly, Love is like fire because it is a great source of energy. Fire creates energy and sends it forth in heat that can be felt by those around it. In the same way, Love creates energy (for Love is the presence of the Holy Spirit, and He is the 'Life-giver' of the Trinity). When a person loves, new life is born even in the most trying of life's circumstances. And this energy pouring forth from a heart that loves can be felt by others just as strongly as heat is felt flowing wildly from fire. Lastly, fire enlightens a room. In the same way, Love sheds a light on situations so that people can see truth, therefore making it easier for them to find God.

It is understandable that after 80 years of Satan's oppressing people in Russia that the country has been left as a pile of seemingly lifeless ashes. Not only were people tortured by a fear of being hurt or killed, but the concept of a loving God, a deeper meaning to suffering, and the hope of an afterlife had been stolen from them by Communism. And on top of that, the Russian economy is oppressive to the majority of people living in that country. Not only in the past, but even today people simply cannot find work. Anyone who possibly can afford it has fled the country. And those left behind have absolutely no hope for their future. And yet, such a hopeless situation can be healed simply by the presence of one thing: God's Love returning to the hearts of His people. God still lives among His special people, chosen in Fatima as His Mother's beloved children. God never left Russia, even when the government tried to slam its country's border closed to any mention of His existence. And through God's persistent beckoning (especially through the missionaries sent to her as messengers of His Love), some of the hearts in Russia have been profoundly changed. When one looks at the situation in Russia with human eyes, it may seem devastatingly hopeless. And yet, Jesus taught us that "With God all things are possible…" With God and the power of His Love any human heart can change—can slowly be transformed back into the image God created him to be at the beginning of time. And so, the power of Love is the most important gift a missionary can bring to Russia. The Russians have a saying, "You cannot try to understand Russia; you simply must love her." And this saying is true. It is virtually impossible to understand the complex wounds present in the Russian heart, but Love can help heal such deep, complex wounds. Missionaries are called to bring such Love to the people they serve. They are called to uncover the presence of God's Love already among the people lost in darkness. And only the presence of the Holy Spirit's Love in the heart of a missionary can enflame the fire of perseverance, patience, wisdom, courage, and kindness needed to help change the many hearts who live in this barren land.

The sort of love needed is a Godly Love, which Loves for the sake of Love and not necessarily in order to see fruit. It is true that love begets love and that a missionary who loves naturally calls for those he loves to imitate such love. Yet even if one hopes for his love to set other hearts on fire with love's presence, when a missionary lives authentic love, reciprocation is never a condition for her to give it. St Bernard of Clairvaux once said something to the effect that **love needs no cause beyond itself, nor does it demand fruits; it is its own purpose. I love because I love; I love that I may love...it is not pure, as it desires some return. Pure love has no self-interest. Pure love does not gain strength through expectation, nor is it weakened by distrust.** And so, a missionary is called to give the deepest Love persistently, daily, in everything he or she says and does. By 'inserting Love' everywhere she goes, the hearts frozen in fear will begin to melt and then burn themselves with the presence of God's Love. The stories in this chapter will be simple stories about ordinary missionaries who allowed God's Love to possess them and drive them forward in their work. One must look underneath the simple ordinariness of what is described here to find the great, extraordinary Love that was needed from God in order to embrace such a mission.

Often when the priests, sisters, and I went to the villages, we would simply have Mass for a small group of people there. It was very informal and very cold in the winter. We would meet at a barn, or a village library, or a cultural center or at someone's house. There was one little city not far from Krasnoyarsk that actually had a parish apartment that had a chapel as well as a meeting area, but the rest of the villages were too poor for that. While Father would hear Confessions before Mass, I would set up a table as the altar. Then I would either practice songs with the people or give a short catechesis. I remember the first time one sister and I together went with a priest on a Friday night to a village for Mass. Our Russian was still pretty limited, and on the ride there Father announced to us that he wanted for us to do a short catechesis on 'the Church' while he heard Confessions. All he simply wanted was for us to explain what the 'Church' was—both a building and a body of people and to help them see themselves as a part of the universal Church. Well, I had many times in my life been asked by priests at the last minute to do teachings, and so that did not scare me at all. And the Holy Spirit gave me exactly what to say in this situation. But I hardly knew Russian at all. But the sister did know it. Her language skills, although far from perfect at the time, were much better than my own. She became suddenly worried and afraid and told Father that she could not do that last minute—she had nothing prepared. I tried to help her, telling her that I knew exactly what to say, but I just could not in my poor Russian. I explained the few points that we needed to cover, and then I promised her I would play my guitar and a few Russian songs about church for us to sing. She refused in her fear, but like the first son in the parable of the two sons in Matthew,[18] after refusing she did end up doing a beautiful teaching when we got there. I started out in my poor Russian, and feeling bad for my failing attempts, she joined in and took over (to my joy).

When we would go to the villages, Father would often say the Mass for the previous Sunday (because although the priests did visit some villages on Sunday afternoons, they could not visit them all). Other times, we would pray the Mass for a big feast that had just occurred. I remember that in November I was at eight All Souls Day Masses. It was beautiful to pray with the people of Russia for all their deceased relatives, many of whom had died without the faith. And I was always amazed how very wise in his homilies was the young Claretian Father, who celebrated all eight of these Masses. Many times, a priest will write a homily for a Mass and repeat it over and over regardless of who is at the Mass. But this missionary priest realized that different souls were at each of these Masses and that the Holy Spirit wanted to say different things to each one. Because of this, I also received eight different homilies by

---

[18] Matthew 21:28-31 "*What is your opinion? A man had two sons. He came to the first and said, 'Son, go out and work in the vineyard today.' He said in reply, 'I will not,' but afterwards he changed his mind and went. The man came to the other son and gave the same order. He said in reply, 'Yes, sir,' but did not go. Which of the two did his father's will?*"

him for the All Soul's Day Mass. I remember also being at five or six Masses with him for Trinity Sunday that year, as well as for the feast of Christ the King and Divine Mercy Sunday. And at each of these as well, he listened to the Holy Spirit and allowed Him to speak through him new things at each place we went. All this attentiveness and care for the souls entrusted to him was a great work of faithful love.

I was very busy my first year in Siberia, jumping around from villages to retreats and then to other cities to help with Masses. I traveled a lot, and my days were long. Sometimes, I would go with the priest only in the evenings, leaving at 3:00 or 4:00 pm and returning home at 10:00 or 11:00 pm. But other times we would go for the whole day. This was rare, since we usually had to meet after the villagers' workdays were finished. Yet, for example, once a week there would be catechesis at a school, and then another meeting in another village as soon as school was let out. I described a typical day in the villages with Father when I wrote a letter home:

The past week I've spent a lot of time in the villages with one of the priests who heard Masses and did catechism. I love the faith of these simple poor village people. Last Wednesday I spent the entire day traveling around with him. We started out in Krasnee Paxar. In this little village, the teachers in the school allow for us to come in for an hour every week and have catechism classes with the kids.[19] I was amazed at what a beautiful job Father did with the kids teaching them the story of the Israelites. He taught about 20-30 kids. As I've said before, these kids are totally uncatechised and so he's got his work cut out for them. Their faces lit up as we pulled up to the schoolhouse building, as some ran around the car throwing snowballs at us. After class we ate lunch at one of the babushkas before we headed off to the second village.

The second village is Startseva. I might have told you before that this is the village where almost everyone is almost always drunk. They are very poor. We had Mass and then catechesis in the village 'club'. Yes, a make-do disco. We had no heat, and during the catechism when we heard a rustling in the corner of the room, Father said, "Don't worry, it's just rats." Yes, we truly celebrated Mass in Bethlehem. It is so sad that these people don't even have a house of worship and so we have to hear Mass in a dance club. Twice while we were there, babushkas came barging in drunk yelling or asking things. Many times, during Mass people disrupted everything, but Father and I just pushed on through (kind of like Youth City[20] days in Texas). We had a catechism afterward on the Ten Commandments.

---

[19] Usually, some sisters went with Father to teach at the school, but, in their absence, father had to teach it alone.

[20] Youth City was the name of the Juvenile Detention Home (jail for teenagers) in Texas where I had volunteered during weekends the year before I came to Siberia.

We are trying to prepare the kids in these villages for the Sacraments. During our catechism, the lights went out on us, and already being dark outside, (and inside our building), we called it a class and headed to the next village.

The last Mass we had was at Solnichi, which is actually a suburby-type place of Krasnoyarsk. It is where they will be building a new church soon. We set up Mass in the apartment that the 'parish' there has. I was excited when a family with lots of kids came (they have 8 kids) and the littlest one climbed all over everyone during Mass... just like home for me. When I returned home (almost 10:00 pm—and I left at 10:00 am), another priest was still at our apartment finishing up the Catholic 12-step meeting with Sister. Their group is growing in number and continuity as well, and so thank you for the prayers!!! They just received a bunch of books and other literature from AA in Moscow, and so we now have a Russian AA Library in our apartment.[21]

And I continued on later in the letter:

On Tuesday, I headed off again with a priest to Arae for Catechesis and Sosnovoborsk for Mass. Arae was great, maybe 12 kids showed up. We meet in this really bare, unheated building, and so we started by singing and dancing...everyone was warm and less timid after Father's silly, holy songs. Even

---

[21] December 5, 2001.

the little guys stayed for all of his teaching on the Ten Commandments (they may be as young as 4). I took pictures of them all bundled up in their big-ol' Russian winter clothes and hats, sitting on a bench, listening to Father teach. His topic this week was how to do the Sign of the Cross, as well as some basic things on the Ten Commandments. These kids really do not know anything. The little guys begged him to 'play the alleluia song' and they sang their little hearts out when he did. I just can't explain to you what hope and joy I have for the Church in Russia, and the whole world when I'm with these kids.

Afterward we drove to Sosnovoborsk for Mass in their 'cultural center'. There was a new, young guy at Mass, and after Mass we started talking. He's got a great story. He was a drug-

addict in Krasnoyarsk for a while, and one day someone came up to him and said that Jesus loved him. He didn't even really know who Jesus was. But a few days later someone again said to him, that if he didn't believe that Jesus loved him, he could die (from the life he was living). He said that in that moment Jesus opened his eyes and his whole life was changed. He immediately stopped his lifestyle with drugs and began to search for Christ—talk about a direct hit by the Holy Spirit!! Right now, he works closely with the Lutherans in Sosnovoborsk with the young people. He said that people in the city know of him and call him and his friends to pray (especially for healing) often. He said that he thinks it is ridiculous that Christian religions are split, and so he tries to work with all of them and unite them. He was really on fire, the kind of fire that only the Holy Spirit could light. Alexei was his name. Please pray for him. He is hope. He is a witness to the power of Jesus' love. I am always amazed when I meet these people here that Jesus Himself has touched and transformed.

And so today was

another 12-hour non-stop crazy day in the villages with Father. We did the same Krasnee Paxar, Startseva, Solnichni route, with an hour stop in Arae that we squeezed in for a funeral. This was my first Russian 'funeral' service. The man who died is named Egor and you can all pray for his soul, if you would be so kind. He looked about 40 years old. They had a casket opened with his body in a back room of his house. About 40 people were squished in there (in the back room, not in the casket ☺). They had already prayed a rosary when we arrived, and so Father just prayed funeral prayers for him. As I looked around the dim room in the middle of the service, I was once more astounded by my life. Here I was in this little dirty, dingy back room of a house in a village in the middle of Siberia praying with a group of babushkas for this man who had died. Maybe you would have to see it to understand how amazing my life is. These people are truly hidden treasures from God!![22]

On one occasion, a Russian sister (who often went with the priests to the villages because she could do catechesis easily in her native Russian tongue), Father, and I went to a village named Arae for a children's catechesis. It was so cold that day that Sister had thought that no one would show up (since it was minus 30 and the building where we met did not have heat), but we were pleasantly surprised when seven or eight kids came. Two new little boys were included in their number (they were around 11 or 12 years old),

---

[22] December 5, 2001.

boys who had never before come to 'learn about God.' These little boys were so excited about our catechesis lesson that they kept interrupting Sister the entire time she taught, drilling her with questions. They were literally jumping out of their seats in excitement about their thoughts and consulting with each other about her answers (discussing amongst themselves whether or not they should believe all this teaching about Jesus). They were genuinely interested and excited. They would say, "Well, I'm just not sure if I believe this. Explain to me why....." and then they attentively listened to the answers. Many of their questions had to do with witchcraft and 'good magic,' for they had heard many stories about people 'healed' by good magic, and they did not understand why it was wrong if it 'helped' people. Sister answered their questions very directly, but in love. And because she was

Russian, language was not a barrier in explaining all this. At one point they were dumbfounded when Sister told them that they could be priests someday. They had never thought of that. In the end, they said they would think about coming back to catechism another time. And although I did not see them again, I have to believe that God had lit a flame in their hearts the first time in bringing them, and that He would nurture that flame into a large fire.

When this Sister was out of town, I always accompanied the priests to the villages so that they would have some help in his work. Yet when this Sister was planning to go, sometimes I went with them and other times I did not. Usually, I simply prayed and tried to listen to what Jesus wanted from me on each given day. Well one day I was not planning to go with them. I was not feeling very well, and so after Sister and I prayed in the morning I went back to bed for a couple of hours. Yet, I was woken up around 12:00 by Jesus, and He told me that He wanted for me to go with Father and Sister that afternoon. I knew that they had already left for the entire day at 11:00 am, and they usually never came back until 9:00 pm at night when all of their various missions were completed. Yet, Jesus told me that I needed to get dressed and go to the Claretian monastery because He wanted me to go with them. Although I doubted His voice (because my reason told me that they had already left), I obeyed. I went over and began to pray in the chapel. I had this burning fire in my heart, for I felt like Jesus really wanted me with them. And I felt guilty that maybe He had told me that earlier (when I still could have obeyed) but I had not listened well enough. Well, shortly after I began praying, I heard this priest's familiar footsteps outside the chapel door. I heard him take his sandals off (only he had sandals with Velcro), and my heart jumped in shock that he was still there. When he came into the chapel, I told him what had happened. He simply smiled. He told me that they went to the village that morning, but that the babushka where they usually ate lunch was not there, so they came back to the monastery to eat before leaving for the next village. He told me to of course come with them.

When we arrived at the village, we set everything up as normal. Father was speaking with Sister and another girl in a corner, and then Sister came up and asked me to be the godmother for this 14-year-old girl's Baptism that day. She said that there was no believing adult Catholic in the village (who was sober) to be her godmother. The girl had been planning for Baptism for a long time, but most of the adults in her village were unbelieving alcoholics. The few babushkas that came to Mass could not read or hear, and they were unkind to the children. Sister's superior had a rule that she could never be a godmother (because she was a missionary and could not promise to stay in touch with a godchild), and so there was no one to be the godmother. I said that I had to talk with Father. I told him that I would, but that I also was a missionary and could not promise to stay in touch with the girl if I moved from Siberia. Father said he understood the situation, and that this was an exception and so he said that not only would he allow me to do it, but that he asked me to please do it. She needed a godmother for Baptism, and she had no one. And so, since I had no official rule forbidding me from doing it, I agreed. Father asked me to take my new godchild, Antonina, and to talk with her a little bit before Mass. We spoke, yet I felt like I could give her so little in such a short time. She truly would be Mary's child, and Mary Herself would have to come and form her. And so, we had the Baptism. I tried on several occasions to make it back to the village to visit her, yet she was only there one time when I came and so we talked very rarely. Yet at her friend's house I left for her two packages with rosaries, books, catechisms, holy cards, bibles, statues of Our Lady and scapulars. I left her everything that I would normally want my godchild to receive from me over many years in life. Because she lived off in this small village, she had no address where I could write her. And so, I simply gave her to Jesus so that He could love and care for her, and I trust that she receives more grace from my life with Him than from the words I would speak to her if I could.

As I have already said, I really enjoyed working in the villages with these priests. Yet it was truly a challenge I had never had before once winter hit that year. Most of the buildings where we had Mass were unheated, and I really struggled to play guitar during the Masses. On a few occasions I simply could not as my fingers were too cold, and on these occasions, Father offered to do it himself (as he was much more talented and warm-blooded than I). Because it was so cold in these villages, I really had to bundle up with lots of long underwear and layers and layers of clothes. It was always colder in the villages than in the city, and in the city, it was between negative 30 and negative 40 degrees. We had to use special

Vaseline on our face so that the blood would not freeze in our cheeks. And we needed to wear several layers of socks with heavy boots. There was one really funny time I will never forget when it was so cold that our water in our Mass kit actually froze in the car on our way to Mass (we had a very poor, little car with bad heat.) This was the same night that my feet froze so badly as we drove that I totally lost feeling in them. We had to stop at a babushka's house and ask for her to allow me to sit by her wood burning stove to warm my feet before we continued. I wrote home once about this:

Well, tonight I went with one of the priests to one of the villages for Mass, and after an hour drive with the heat on high all of our windows were still covered with ice, and (it gets better) when we opened the suitcase with the Mass kit to set up for Mass, the little container of water had frozen on our drive. Don't worry, I've adapted. We even bought some of the cream here that people need to put on their face so that their blood doesn't freeze in their cheeks. It has been negative 20's and 30's here this week, and when I was in Achinsk on Monday it even was supposed to hit negative 40 (I'm not sure if it did.)   But with two or sometimes three pairs of long underwear under clothes, it's manageable.[23]

---

[23] December 14, 2001.

On the rare occasion, the Claretians would go to the home of a homebound Catholic in Krasnoyarsk to say Mass for them. One Monday afternoon, I went into the chapel at the Claretians to pray, and within an hour or so I saw that one of the Claretians was getting things together for a travel Mass. That week in particular it was very cold (-40's) and so instead of walking (or running) my 45 minutes to Mass, I often simply got a ride to church with one of the priests. (I did not take the bus because it was a needless expense and often as I stood waiting for it, I froze more than if I simply ran to Mass). This father told me that he would be leaving early for Mass, for he had to go to a woman's house for a house Mass, and he invited me to come along to minister to her (yet he warned me that it would be difficult). I felt strongly like Jesus wanted for me to go, although I myself did not really want to (as I was nervous in trying to communicate with people I did not know well in my poor Russian). Yet Jesus gave many graces to me and to others in this simple, hidden visit. When we arrived at the lady's apartment, I saw that the woman was bound to her wheelchair and bed—maybe even paralyzed. I wrote home:

> Monday afternoon I got to go with one of the priests to celebrate Mass in a lady's apartment here in Krasnoyarsk. She is in a wheelchair and quite sickly, and so cannot make it out to church. While Father was hearing her Confession, I made my way out of the living room (where they were) and into the kitchen, where another lady was (maybe her daughter). I began talking with her as I waited for the Confession to end. She

asked me where I was from (my accent always gives me away) and if I was Catholic. Her response was, 'Oh, I'm Orthodox.' I said, 'That's great. You know we have got the same Jesus, the same Father, the same Holy Spirit, and the same Momma Mary.' She kinda smiled and said, 'Yeah, I guess so.' Although she was kinda shy at first, we had a great conversation while she prepared dinner and worked on knitting some woolen stockings simultaneously. (I was impressed.) In the end, she asked me to come back. You know, it's in the apartment kitchens of Russia where union between the Orthodox and Catholics will be realized...one heart at a time.[24]

---

[24] December 14, 2001

Kansk

In addition to helping out in Krasnoyarsk, Sister and I would travel twice a month to a city called Kansk, 250 km from Krasnoyarsk. The parish there was called Most Holy Trinity Parish, and it was the parish that the Bishop had originally assigned to SOLT to take on as their own before Fr. Tom (the priest who was to be the head of our Russian mission team) got sick. The Claretians had been caring for this parish for quite some time and were planning to hand it off to SOLT whenever a priest could arrive. In the meantime, Sister and I traveled with them to serve the needs of this little parish every other weekend.

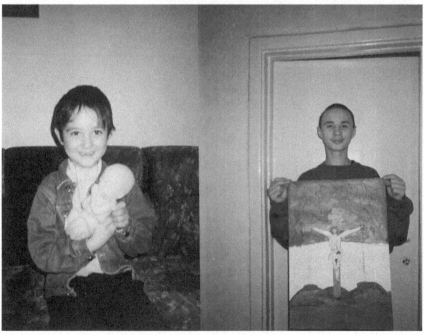

Kansk was a very poor town, in many respects. The streets were especially atrocious. For example, when they did construction of the streets, they simply ripped up the whole road and all the cars needed to drive straight through the construction anyway (and most of the city is 'under construction,' yet never gets constructed). The road in the back of our apartment building had a 20-foot deep, 15-foot across hole to the sewage system. This 'road construction' had been going on for a couple of years when I got there and had not been finished when I left two years later. The city often did not have hot or cold water (in Russia, it was not uncommon to lose either hot or cold water in the apartments, but usually not both). Most people were out of work (I was told by the parishioners that about 90% of the people were out of work). The city was centered

around two factories—one that made vodka (and often sold illegally strong vodka—like rubbing alcohol—to people, which sometimes killed them), and the other that made cigarettes. The town was very quiet. I was struck by that quietness every time we visited. Although the parishioners in Kansk were often embarrassed about their city (saying that it was quiet and boring compared to Krasnoyarsk), I always thought that the poverty (in addition to the quietness of the place) left much room for the quiet voice of God to work among His people there. It was a good place for prayer—it had an empty silence, but an empty silence waiting to be filled with His Life and Love. The people of the city are almost all Polish or Ukrainian exiles from the days of Communism when they were 'sent to Siberia' as punishment for 'crimes against

the people.' I heard many stories in Kansk from Babushkas and older men retelling their memories of when they were sent there as children, torn from their families. These people were often Catholic, and so they held on to the faith secretly even in the midst of the dark Communist eye watching to 'catch'

them. Like most of the Catholics in Siberia, they had deep roots, yet their roots were weak. They held on to the secret tradition of the faith as their families passed it down, yet most of the time their faith consisted of saying a few prayers that their grandmothers had taught them (and that they, in turn, taught their grandchildren in secret) and of secret baptisms of the children at night. During the years of Communism, some of these believers had 'friends' visit from Poland, who were actually priests in laymen's clothes, and they had secret Masses at night in their homes. Because they were forbidden by the communists to believe in God or to practice their faith, most of these Catholics in Kansk were extremely uncatechised, yet hungry for knowledge about God.

This parish in Kansk had a very interesting history. They were one of the first groups of Catholics to come together after the fall of Communism. The core of this parish was a Polish family, whose mother had been very strong in the faith during Communism. She had many children, and these children and their children made up most of the parish. Even during Communism, this matriarch would lead a weekly 'liturgy' service consisting of reading scriptures. And her job was also to baptize the children (and grandchildren). When we started to visit Kansk, one of this woman's daughters was living in her house (as she has died) and told us that she remembered being 3 years old, the windows being closed and drapes drawn, as a small community gathered to pray. Sometimes, they had secret Masses prayed in her living room at night by visiting priests. In 1991, when things became a little freer in Russia, this woman's house was where they celebrated Mass with mission priests. Even the present Bishop of Western Siberia had been to that house. This woman even showed us on one occasion all of her mother's pictures of Mary and Jesus which were kept hidden away all those years.

The Claretian priests had been coming to Kansk on every other Saturday in time to have Mass at the parish apartment at 5:00 pm, with some sort of tea and cookies afterwards. Sunday morning, they would have Mass at a music school that rented a room out to us and following that the priests would often go over to one of the parishioners' houses for a meal before the drive home. Yet with a new priest we changed that a bit. The people cried to us the first time we were there, begging for more catechesis. They were very hungry for the faith, and they wanted more time with us. So, we decided to come in on Friday night (which was difficult for father to drive 3-5 hours—depending on the roads) after a long day in Krasnoyarsk. This way we could plan some sort of catechesis for the people for Saturday evening before or after our rosary and Mass. And Sundays after Confession and Mass father sometimes gave a teaching to the adults, Sister started catechesis with the little kids, and after all that the three of us went back to the parish apartment for a 4-hour long youth group with the young adults. I felt especially bad when the parishioners pressured father into coming over for dinner after all that, and after 3 ½ hours of conversation he needed to drive back to Krasnoyarsk exhausted. I loved these women parishioners, and I understood that they just wanted our love and presence, but they were a bit controlling, and I had to strive to really love them and not be frustrated with them when they exerted their manipulating ways on poor, tired father. They would become jealous of the children if we gave them too much attention and they would try for us to not have children's catechesis so that we could eat lunch with them. In the end, the priest decided to of course stay with our schedule of youth group and work with the children, but also try to squish in dinner after it all. We would arrive home at 12:00 am, sometimes, on those Sunday nights. I simply offered up being with these ladies and prayed that father would not fall asleep on our drive home (while we talked to him to keep him awake).

I tried to see the desire of the parish ladies to eat with us as a desire for God, for goodness, and for love. And they said that they wanted to learn from us while we ate—sometimes they asked us theological questions during dinner. And it was beautiful to see the great hunger and thirst these people had for God and for religious things these first months we were there. In working in the missions, usually half the job is to give people thirst or hunger before it is filled. People need to thirst, to really want God, in order to receive the Gospel message. In Kansk, the ground seemed to be tilled, the job half done. Father tried to encourage them to appreciate what they had and to make good use of it, as opposed to complaining that they did not have more. I would come to see how wise were his words, for a year-and-a-half later when SOLT would permanently move to Kansk and offer the possibility of more catechesis, their original enthusiastic desire would not play out in their concrete lives—as they hardly came. And so, in these first trips we simply tried to make the short time we had with them quality time full of Jesus' great love, and then we gave them to Mary as we continued on back to Krasnoyarsk and the next villages to work.

The first time that Sister, Father, and I went to Kansk together was to bring the traveling Fatima statue there for prayer. We went on a Monday as opposed to a weekend, for the statue had needed to be in Krasnoyarsk for the weekend. I remember how in that short few hours we were there how I had a beautiful experience. I had visited Kansk once that previous summer with a different priest (before this new priest was assigned as the official Kansk priest), and I had met some young neighbor boys. On this return trip a couple of months later, Jesus led me to meet up with these little, neighbor boys again. This is what happened:

When I visited [Kansk] this past Monday, I met up with some little boys who I had met a few months ago outside our apartment. Misha is a 6-year-old going on 27. How I originally met him and his little 1-year-old brother is a story and a half. The first time I visited Kansk in July, I looked out our 5th floor window below at the street with a huge sewage hole, as I explained above, and saw a few little boys playing near this crevice. They were throwing rocks into the sewage to watch them splash. And then I saw this baby, who was placed alone on a huge sewage pipe a few feet away to 'watch' his brother; and he was getting quite antsy. He was trying to slide off of the pipe (about a 4 ft drop) to join his brother, who at this point was climbing INTO the hole. Well, despite my hesitations of not wanting to interfere with another culture's ways (the way children are raised here is much different), all my motherly instincts won, and I grabbed Sister and ran down to the ditch. When I got there, we had to climb through sewage to reach the boys (it was quite interesting), and I grabbed the baby who thought standing on this pipe four feet off the ground and next to a 15-20 ft hole was just fine. Obviously, the 'big brother' wanted to discuss this with me. After drilling me with questions on where I was from, and did I train or fly from America, he answered my question of, "Don't you think you need to be a little more careful with your little brother?" All he said to me in his macho little voice (I mean this little guy was tough) was, "Well, lady, you know he's never fallen before." After Sis and I stood around long enough monitoring the situation, his babysitting pride was bothered, and he decided maybe we were right, and he moved his brother a little further away.

And then, here I met him again Monday, a good two months later, outside our apartment. After another series of 20 questions of 'Where have you been?' and 'When will you move here?' he said to me, "You know, I didn't pray for you." (I had asked him to pray for me.) And before I could ask him why, he offered the explanation: "I don't need to pray. I have everything I need. I don't need God." Now, by looking at this little guy (and seeing that his mother didn't care much after him or his brother) I KNEW that necessity had aged him and as a defense mechanism he 'wasn't allowed to need anything.' We talked a bit more, his little friends said that they prayed every day and would pray for me, and I left. Unfortunately, many children here become adults quickly...many adults say they never had a childhood. Please pray especially for Misha and his brother.[25]

The first few times we began to regularly go to Kansk for Mass (as the Claretians had *tried* to go twice a month, but had actually not been there for a couple of months), 8 people came to the Saturday night Mass and maybe 15 to the Sunday morning Mass. We had heard that the parish had been much larger than that, but as they never knew exactly when a priest was coming, they got out of the habit of attending Mass on Sundays. Yet as we began to come regularly (and Father began to shepherd them beautifully), more and more people began to come. I think that they responded so beautifully to Father because of his deep love for them. Many of them told me that they felt loved by him and so they were not afraid (as Russians usually feared God, and often feared men in general). Father noticed after a few months of going that although almost 40 people came on Sunday mornings for Mass (half of them under 20 years old), most of them were not going to Communion. After Mass when the priest usually would give announcements, Father had a little talk with the people about the importance of Confession and of receiving Jesus in the Eucharist at Mass if possible. He wanted to know why people were not receiving Jesus, and he asked them what he could do to help. He asked if they were

---

[25] October 9, 2001

they afraid of Confession, or if maybe they wanted a different priest to come to hear Confessions. They all yelled 'no,' that they did not want another priest. They loved him. So, he asked them then why they did not want Confession and to receive Jesus. He said that he realized that a few of them could not receive Jesus because of their present life situations, but most of the problem was that the people just did not like Confession—and so they did not go. It was beautiful that they realized that they should not receive Jesus in Communion if they had committed mortal sins and did not go to Confession. Father really worked with them on this problem of fear so that they would go to Confession and then receive Jesus. He said that Jesus was dying to give Himself to them, to give them comfort, strength, love, and healing. He said that coming to Mass and refusing Confession beforehand, and therefore Communion at Mass, was like going to dinner at someone's house and refusing to eat.

Well, a month later we started Mass 2 HOURS LATE because of how many Confessions Father had to hear. His talk a month earlier about the importance of Confession and receiving Communion at Mass had really hit some buttons because two weeks after it when we returned to Kansk he heard Confessions for an hour on Saturday and an hour on Sunday, and the following weekend we came he heard them for two hours straight on Sunday. We prayed a rosary while we waited for him to finish, and then sister and I tried to play every Russian song we knew on the guitar to sing with the people while we waited for Mass. I remember worrying a little when Father did not come out for Mass for two hours because I knew he had been exhausted when we arrived for Mass. (He had had to sleep in the car all night because it was 40 below zero and if we turned the car off, it would never turn on again. If we would have left the car running, someone would have stolen it. And so, Father simply had to sleep in it. Although he had a sleeping bag, I knew he had not slept well.) Anyway, as I thought as a human does, I worried about him being tired, yet when he came in for Mass, he was glowing with the Holy Spirit from the graces of hearing so many Confessions. It gave me so much joy to see such grace, and I learned a great lesson in that about the power of God's love in Confession.

After Mass on Sunday, we began to meet at the apartment for a youth group. Because most of the kids were coming from Mass, they had not eaten and would be hungry for lunch. Sister wanted to be the cook, so father asked me to help him run the meetings with the kids. The first meeting we had 20 teenagers show up. We each told a bit about ourselves and father taught them a few songs on the guitar. He asked them what they wanted out of the group, how long they wanted the meetings (they said all day because they did not want to go home), and what topics they were interested in learning about. Then we had a break. After the break Father gave them a little talk on the angels and the devil. We broke into groups after that to answer questions together. Somehow, the group father assigned to me ended up being a few girls (with seemingly moral foundations) and all the guys who had not known that they were going to a youth group meeting before they showed up to the apartment (they just followed their friends) and who did not really

believe in God. I simply prayed that the love of God surrounding them somehow helped their souls grow in a thirst for Him a little. After our small groups, our dear Sister had 'whipped together' a quick dinner for 25 people (God bless her quick creative energies) and we all ate together. Then those who wanted to stay could watch a video on people's religious lives in Siberia. I was happily surprised that out of the 10 people who stayed, all the unbelieving guys in my group were among them!! Maybe they had nowhere else to go, but I still hoped that Jesus was somehow drawing them to Himself.

We began little by little to extend and deepen the prayer life of the parishioners on these short weekend visits to Kansk. We always were prepared early so that we could pray a rosary and also have

Confessions before Mass on Saturday evening. We also began to have adoration with the parishioners for 10 or 15 minutes after Mass. This was very new for them. And it was amazing for me to sit with Jesus and to praise, adore, and love Him knowing that His Eucharistic presence was nowhere else within a few hours of us (we were the only Catholic 'mission' in the 1000 km stretch between Krasnoyarsk and Irkutsk). Father also kept a host after the Saturday evening Mass so that Sister and I could have adoration after the parishioners left. I would pray for hours, and Jesus gave my heart much comfort in the vacuum of darkness I felt around me in Kansk.

So much work went into such little things in the work of evangelization in Russia. Problems seemed to constantly be arising. One night on a long drive to another city for a retreat our car broke down because we had been sold water instead of gas. On another occasion we would have no water for a week at a time. In another situation, we would have to drive for hours through terrible blizzards in order to say a Mass at a village, only for one person to show up when we arrived. It was true that at times we also encountered situations in Russia that were difficult, and the country's problems were not always understandable, but the power of Jesus' faithful Love always was enough to push us forward in our mission. And I truly believe that the little seeds of love that we planted throughout the land of Siberia, one day would be watered by others and eventually would bloom into great, beautiful fruit for God.

Chapter 6

Jesus' Patient Heart on the Cross

"If you seek patience, you will find no better example than the cross. Great patience occurs in two ways: either when one patiently suffers much, or when one suffers things which one is able to avoid and yet does not avoid. Christ endured much on the cross, and did so patiently, because when he suffered he did not threaten; he was led like a sheep to the slaughter and he did not open his mouth."
-St. Thomas Aquinas

Jesus' Heart on the Cross was very patient. If one meditates on this a moment, he will see how silly our impatience in suffering often is. As Jesus hung on the Cross, He simply 'Fiated'. He did not try to stop the people from killing Him—He just surrendered in trust of His Father. He was so patient with humanity—and even offered forgiveness to those who crucified Him. And, in the end, this patient endurance of Jesus won for us salvation. In the same way, my mission life in Russia called me to imitate Jesus' patience on the Cross. If I would have wanted to see fruit, I would have been frustrated. If I would have expected those I served to respond immediately to me in kindness, understanding, or love, I would have given up. What I needed to do is constantly look to Jesus on the Cross—to how He brought His Father's Love to humanity through the Cross—and strive to imitate it. Jesus focused on His Father, and because of His union with Him (even when He did not feel or see Him, they were united in obedience) He was able to keep His heart patient and peaceful even in the midst of the most difficult tribulations. Jesus' love on the Cross did not have limits. He simply absorbed everything that happened to Him and remained faithful unto death. Jesus asked me to imitate His Love in this way—absorbing all I met in Russia and striving to remain faithful unto death. The direst circumstances call for the direst love—and as I strove to open myself up in surrender to Jesus, He gave me the grace I needed to continue on in love, when humanly I was tired, discouraged and ready to give up.

I most desperately needed to draw from Jesus' crucified patience when I visited Siberia in November of 2005. I was disappointed to find the situation had worsened in many places in the two years since I had left. And in those places where the spiritual lives of the people had deepened a bit, very few flowers could be seen from the seeds we had tirelessly planted in hearts two years earlier. I also found myself dealing with situations much more 'hopeless' than I had ever encountered before. Here are some examples of such situations. I wrote about it in letters to friends and family at home:

...There is a woman from the parish here who is living at the monastery. She has no family except her little sister who is 25. She allowed her little sister to move in her apartment with her when her sister got pregnant with her first baby (the girl is not married)... She now has two little boys (from different fathers). Last night this sister told me that she was a prostitute for many years, but her sister does not know this. Anyway, she is really wounded (they both are, but the older one tries to pray, and her younger sister is very closed to God). The younger one drinks a lot and when she gets drunk she beats people up. She beat her older sister up, and that is why she came to live here at the monastery. The neighbor lady called here last night and said that she beat the neighbor lady and that she locked her baby (5 months old) and little boy (who is 3) in the apartment and left them. So, this older sister, Sister T and I went to the apartment to see the children. This woman hates her blood sister (who kindly allows them to live with her) and also hates Sister (because she has told her that she needs to change her life). She loves me, though (we really do not know why), and so I can work with her a little bit because of that... I only met her twice before this in Russia, once when she was pregnant with her first little boy and again about 9 months later—both times she was drunk, but we prayed together. When we arrived, she was already back at home (we had been called because she had abandoned the children), and she remembered me and was very happy to see me. She was too drunk to take care of her kids but would not let anybody touch them except me... and she said she wanted to talk with me. She begged me to stay the night. I did not want to stay at all, but Jesus told me that I should and that I should not be afraid. He was very strong in my heart and in love. This woman told me all about her life and sins—I was only sad that I could not absolve them... she said she was too big of a sinner for anyone to forgive her, even God, and she was too embarrassed to tell a priest. I was glad I stayed because I just prayed all night and when the baby woke up wet and crying and hungry the mom was hung-over sleeping from being drunk and would not get up to help him—so I did. The baby smelled like bathroom and the house smelled like vodka and smoke... it was horrible. But what was worse was that these children live like this always. There are so many in Russia like this—I just forgot how sad the situation is here... it was interesting too because she had this baby right after Johnny[26] died. She named him Evan, she said, after Johnny and the Pope (even though she does not really believe in God). I took this as

---

[26] Johnny is my brother, who died in a tragic car accident when he was 20 years old.

a beautiful sign and prayed asking for their help last night. It is just so dark... but I feel Jesus so strong with me.

It breaks my heart that in Russia there is no program like there is in Poland or the US where if a mom is drunk and beats kids that they take the children away and let someone else care for them... it is just a very serious and sad thing... When we call the police to report that this woman is drunk and locked her kids in the house crying, the police show up drunk and say, "So what? So, this woman got drunk once. Everyone gets drunk sometimes..." And they do not do anything to help the children.

Last night was really hard for me. This woman's sister got drunk again and fell asleep and her little boy and baby screamed for several hours... we could not get into the apartment to help them because the door was locked from the inside and the little boy was not strong or tall enough to open it. In the end, this woman's sister somehow climbed from the neighbor's balcony into a window she broke. Those poor children. Their 'mother' slept passed out drunk for like 7 hours and then woke up and was mad we were there. She never said she felt bad or was wrong in drinking. She never said anything. I think she is psychologically ill... Anyway, it is crazy in Russia because we can't do anything for these children. The police won't take them away from her unless she wants them to do it. And they don't care that she is drunk all the time and like today she fell asleep for 7 hours while the kids screamed. The baby fell on his face during that time... they could have died. Anyway, this woman's sister is a mess. She just cries and

cries and lies in bed. She only said two sentences to me last night—
'Where is God in all this?' and *'I don't want to live'.* My heart is
broke for her. I just have no idea how to help. I have nothing to say
that can help... she is holy in how she tries to love her sister anyway
(even if her sister says she wants to kill her)... What can I say to
her? How can I help? I can help only in my fiat love with Jesus—
only by striving to be faithful to my vocation...

October 30, 2005
Dear family,
May Jesus bless you all with His Great Love!!
So, I am sorry I have not been able to write you guys more
until now. I actually feel like I speak with you every day since I
pray for you all so much. Yet I know that a few of you have
mentioned that you have not heard from me for a while, and so
I thought I would drop you all a note (sorry I cannot write 60
individual letters) to let you know where I am and how I am.
As you know, I spent the last month visiting Siberia. It was
wonderful to be back there. I love Russia, even though it is very
difficult to love. I think I love it so much because it is like a
great cold, barren desert—there is such a need for love there. It
is like if you met a little, abandoned, shivering child in the
street you could not help but love him, help him... Russia is like
that with my heart... Its pitifulness just calls forth great love. I
saw during my month stay how bad the situation in Russia still
is. Although there were some little signs of light, growth,
miracles, in general the situation there is worse than before. In

Krasnoyarsk there are no more beggars anywhere on the streets—this really surprised me since there used to be several on every street corner. I know that the rich are richer now than before, but the economic life of the 'normal everyday Russian' has not gotten that much better. When I mentioned this to the other missionaries, we all agreed it was a bit strange that all the beggars in St. Petersburg, Krasnoyarsk, and Magadan disappeared almost overnight. As I began to ask the Russians about this, their answers were similar to our missionary friends'... the 'gut' is that these beggars were rounded up and either sent somewhere or killed. They always were a bit controlled by a mob-type system—answering to someone and giving a portion of what they received each day to someone who offered 'protection,' and we fear now they were simply gotten rid of. One good thing in Krasnoyarsk was that I met about 12 or 13 new little faces at the parish—in the two years I have been gone some young families have found the courage to begin to have children again. We never had little ones at the parish before (maybe a visitor for a bit or one American family I knew had a child), but Russians were afraid to have children in such a bad situation. Now they have stepped forth and begun to have little ones again—these children will be the first generation born into the Church and raised with a normal relationship with God. And so, this was a bit of hope. One more beautiful thing in Achinsk that I saw was that the parishioners requested that the first Friday of the month that they have all night adoration—each person taking an hour and spending the rest of the night sleeping at the parish retreat house (they can't travel to and from home like in America because most have no car and public transportation does not work late at night).

In many other ways, though, I was saddened for Russia and reminded of our deep need for prayer for Russia's conversion. I was reminded of Jesus' words in Matthew 12:43-45: *"When an unclean spirit goes out of a person it roams through arid regions searching for rest but finds none. Then it says, 'I will return to my home from which I came.' But upon returning, it finds it empty, swept clean, and put in order. Then it goes and brings back with itself seven other spirits more evil than itself, and they move in and dwell there; and the last condition of that person is worse than the first. Thus it will be with this evil generation."* I never understood this passage well until Russia—to me it is very clear that just this has begun to happen there. When God casts evil from a person or a home or a country that person (or people) must fill what has be emptied with God and His Life and Love. They must fill what was emptied of evil with a life of goodness... The 'demon' of Communism was 'cast out' of Russia, but because they had not filled that empty space quickly enough with God (at no fault of their own, many times, for they did not know better) many other 'demons' have entered their society—a great demon of alcoholism, prostitution, pornography, witchcraft, etc... Their entire society is falling apart. I know that they had some of these problems during Communism, but in a more hidden way—yet now it is in the streets. Drunken people passed out all over the streets—pornography on billboards, etc... prostitutes line the streets at night...In the bigger cities it is not as evident, but in smaller cities and in the villages (where most people live) things are very dark.

For example, everyone is drunk. It is not a funny drunk—it is a sickening drunkenness that kills people... I wrote most of you asking for prayers for that woman on the night I spent with her children when she was drunk. A few days before I left, she got so drunk again that she passed out and after her little children (3 years old and 7 months) screamed and cried for a few hours the neighbor climbed through his balcony and broke a window to get into the apartment to let her sister in to help them (the children were locked in the apartment with their passed out mother). The baby had fallen on his face into a pillow and could have suffocated. The older boy lost his voice from crying. When we arrived, they had already gotten into the apartment, but the woman's sister was afraid of staying there alone because if her sister would have woken up, she had already threatened to kill her... so I stayed with her... The sad thing is that when we have called the police about such matters they either show up drunk themselves or make no big deal about it saying, "Well, what is the big deal? So she got drunk? Everyone does that sometimes." There is no way to help these children because Russia has a clause in her Constitution that the government cannot bother in family matters unless someone is killed... When I came home at 3 am that night after straightening out the situation as much as I could do, I was heartbroken when I saw 4 little boys (who could not have been older than 5 or 6) sitting on a bench in the street. When I asked about this, I was told (by both Russians and the missionaries) that that was normal for that city. They said, "Mary, do you know how many children live in the streets here? In Russia there are 5 million children living like that in the streets." Their parents get drunk, and they don't want to stay home with them... It is just sad. And there are not enough missionaries to help all these kids. There is just so much work there and so few workers.... I was reminded of the Gospels so often: *"The harvest is plenty, but the laborers are few... ask the Master of the harvest to send more laborers into the field..."* (Luke 10:2) and *"At the sight of the crowds, his heart was moved with pity for them because they were troubled and abandoned, like sheep without a shepherd."* (Mt 9:36) Oh, these poor children!

And when you try to help people you don't always get far— how can you help convert a drunk person? how can you help a woman who has lost her conscience totally (she drinks to forget her life and sin and so that she can go work as a prostitute— something she would never do soberly—so that she can make money for more vodka... it is a vicious cycle)... Yet in all this I realized more and more how much simply the presence of prayer is needed in Russia. People who pray will help them more than any social work program—for it is a spiritual battle as much as a physical one there. If someone's heart is frozen cold by sin, wounds, etc... and they refuse to take the gift of Jesus' fiery Love from you, the one thing you can do is hold Jesus' Love and stand near them until their hearts begin to melt a little—and after lots of patience, prayer, and simple Love (and lots of time) they will open to receive Jesus' Love themselves. And so that is the work of missionaries in Russia. Yes, it is very dark and empty there—but we need people to go and live holding Jesus' light in the midst of that... just to live faithful to their lives with God in the midst of these others ... and then that light will slowly begin to move out and ignite others' hearts. Prayer is the most important work in Russia—for without it no one will receive the gift of Love that Jesus wants to share with them. There are so many problems there that Russia needs deep healing—miraculous healing—and that only comes through prayer.

October 29, 2005

...I also see how tired the missionaries are in general. Even the holiest priests are starting to get really down because of the people's lack of response... They do not know how to 'wake up' the young people... everyone is just frozen and lazy in many ways. The many parish groups are way down in numbers... it is just hard. The message I kept getting for everyone as they shared these problems was the same: "Faithfulness, Faithfulness, Faithfulness." They simply needed to remain faithful, and God would do the rest. (Another missionary) also received this strongly in her heart one day at Mass as we prayed together—that the missionaries themselves have to return to the first love they had for Jesus; return to that pure love that does not seek fruit but loves for the sake of love. Oh, Russia is so hard—the land of 'hidden fruit'... just say a prayer or two for our family there so that they persevere and receive the renewal of strength they need.

One good thing, though, is that Krasnoyarsk has had lots of seminars this year—12 steps and other seminars on working with children of alcoholics...

...Although there are some big changes in Krasnoyarsk, unfortunately things are no different (or worse) in the little cities and villages. I traveled to Sosovnaborsk with (Father), and the situation there is just bad. In the villages everyone is drunk. How can you help convert a drunk person? Achinsk is a mess. The parish has grown in little ways—maybe just deeper. it is not much bigger, but the same people faithfully come— even the youth. The parishioners asked the priests last year to start all-night adoration the first Friday of the month. This was their idea, initiative, and they faithfully come and each take an hour to pray (sleeping at the parish house there). That is beautiful. But the city itself is such a mess. I could tell you 1000 horror stories of what I ran into... prostitutes, many little children on the streets, drunkards, murder, abuse, abandoned children. There is no system (that works here) to help children stuck with neglectful or abusive parents unless one of them is killed. I guess Russia has a clause in their constitution that says the government cannot mess in family matters. The evil is just everywhere there. It is so hard to work with these people—how can you help convert a woman who has lost her conscience? You just have to hold Jesus in your heart and stand near her (enduring her sin) until His warmth begins to melt her frozen heart... it is such a long process. I was reminded of how important it is just to have a presence of prayer in Russia—a presence of prayer and lots of patience. Sister Tatiana and I talked about how Achinsk needs 5 or 6 more monasteries of sisters living there—just to have a presence of prayer... Maybe the alcoholism, abuse, pornography (they now have big TVs on the streets in Krasnoyarsk, but the commercials are sometimes naked women), etc., was there before, but it was just hidden; but now the evil is very open—maybe God just has allowed these wounds to be opened up in a visible way so He can heal them... I don't know. All I know is that Russia needs prayer like never before.

The tragedy that I met in Russia was much deeper than I described in these e-mails. There was a little girl at the parish named Kristina. She would often come in at the end of daily Mass and run up to each of the sisters for a hug and then leave. She was about 8 years old (I know she was in the 3rd grade). I asked Sister Tatiana where she came from and she answered that she was a little neighbor girl of one of the parishioners. She had never known her father and her mother abandoned her. She lived with her alcoholic grandparents who neglected her. She was 8 years old, and not only could she not read, but she did not even know her letters. Sister met with her on Saturdays to teach her catechism as well as to teach her the alphabet and how to read. Sister told me about another family at the parish. The parents never attended Mass, but three of their seven children did. Sister said that their parents were also alcoholics who beat their children. She said that they even one time threw one of their little girls out of a fifth story window. Miraculously the child was never hurt (except for some mental slowness). There was also Natolia. His parents were very loving, but both had been raised in an orphanage and so they allowed their two boys to do anything they wanted. For this reason, they were very hyper all the time. Yet, even if these boys had parents who loved them, they still suffered from poverty. I remember one day in Mass Natolia had a cold and his nose was running all over and he kept trying to wipe it in his hands. I handed him a Kleenex and he smiled at me like I had given him the greatest gift in the world. Then he folded it nicely like a treasure and just stared at it—he looked up at me with huge eyes and asked, "What is it?" This child had never seen a Kleenex before! He did not know how to use it either, and so sister and I discreetly tried to teach him during Mass, even though we were sitting in the front pew.

Situations like these overwhelmed me like waves during the four short weeks I visited Siberia that fall. The darkness was so tangible, and I had to fight to keep my heart close with Jesus so that His Light would continue to burn strong even in the midst of the rain and winds of destitution, spiritual desolation, despair, and depression surrounding me. The horrible evil sin and suffering as well as my own weak helplessness to help truly overwhelmed me on the last day I spent in Achinsk before I was to return to Poland:

I leave tomorrow morning for Petersburg. I am so sad, I cried a lot today. I am sad because of all the great suffering and sin here... I am sad because of all the great suffering and sin in the world. People do not open their hearts to Jesus... everything is so dark... it was really hard for me the last two days with that drunk woman and her children... The next day (after we went to her house to help the children because she was drunk and fell asleep and locked the children in the house alone) her sister was in bed all day. She is going to be psychologically sick soon, I fear. She does not eat and only drinks coffee and smokes. And then last night her sister called again (she was drunk) and said that if she did not come to her apartment, she would leave her children alone. She ran there to help the children (her nephews) and her sister left to work as a prostitute all night so that she would have more money to drink. Anyway, there are SO many people like this here... so many children on the streets (like those four little boys I saw at 3 am two nights ago)—and the whole world is just so empty of Jesus' love. I am lonely because of it, or I should say He shares His deep loneliness with me. I just am so overwhelmed. I have been here a month and I see that not only I have not helped anyone really (all the problems are still here) but I failed in so many ways—I spoke when I should have been quiet and was quiet when I should have spoken, or I did not act right to help people in a situation. And I prayed and asked Jesus for help with these sisters (the drunk mother, etc.,)—just to know what to do, and I never heard an answer. He spoke to me about my life, but I could never hear what to do to help her. And I don't even live my vocation well... I try, but I fail, and I see that because I fail so greatly other people suffer. There are so many people suffering in the world and so much sin, and I just cry...

On another occasion I prayed:

I feel strongly in myself the many different and deep ways that Your Heart suffers here among Your people, especially because their love has grown so cold. I simply try to receive Your Heart crucified open to rest in mine. May my heart, although little and weak, be Your comfort and be Your place of rest—rest from all the many sufferings You endure. Please help me always remain open wide in fiat to You. Please come to me, for me—fill me and carry me, my Beloved Spouse! Amen.

Jesus did use such difficult situations to teach me about His Love. He was my only consolation in this month—and yet, He was the only consolation I needed. I remember on two occasions He gave me very concrete answers encouraging me to continue on with His patience on the Cross.

October 4, 2005

"My Jesus," I prayed, "I pray and suffer and I feel Your presence so powerful here with me, but there is absolutely no fruit that I see from this prayer and suffering."

Jesus answered in my heart, **"My Mary, it must be the proper season, the right time of year, in order for a farmer to gather his fruit. It does not matter when he planted or how long or hard he works, fruit does not come forth until its proper season. That is also how it is with My work with souls. I use you, your presence of prayer and suffering to plant many little seeds of My great Love and mercy deep in the hearts of My people here. But you will not see the plant that I allow to grow forth from these seeds. You yourself will not collect or gather such fruit and present it to Me—that will be the work of another. All you are to do is remain faithful in 'fiat' in your night of the Cross with Me. I will do all the rest. You must be more patient with My way, My time, with everything. In the proper season beautiful flowers and wonderful fruits will bloom forth from the work of My Love in you. I simply ask you to remain faithful with Me in fiat. I bless you in this your long day of tired, quiet fiat Love. Amen."**

October 25, 2005

My Jesus, thank you for my vocation. Please help me be faithful to it.

My question of the day, Jesus, is 'How do you convert a person who no longer has a conscience?' My work here in Russia for the last month has brought this question to the surface—it is an experiential question and I need an experiential answer from You, Jesus. How would You work to help these people here?

Jesus answered me with a vision of the Cross. He said, **"Like this:**

With My Heart on the Cross. Through My Heart's suffering crucifixion on the Cross, I enter into these people's deepest, darkest suffering and sin and redeem them. I offer them My redemption from the Cross. Even if their hearts are completely closed to My Love I continue to search out paths to enter in and reach them. I pound, chip and carve away at their hearts—hardened by sin, until I find a place soft and sensitive enough to receive a tiny drop of My Love, of My blood—and this single drop is enough to redeem them. In this single drop of My blood and Love is all the power they need to turn from sin and return to Me. I am a very patient God. Look at My great, patient Love from the Cross. Imitate Me in that patient, faithful Love.

Yes, My missionaries in Russia must have My patience—must allow My patience to enter in and love through them. In order to love others with My patient faithful mercy and Love, they must keep before their heart's eyes their own sinfulness and My endless forgiving, patient merciful Love for them in this. Through their weakness and sin offered to Me on the Cross I will enter them and fill them with My patient Love. This Love is not to simply fill them and lay stagnant in their hearts, but instead is to flow out as patient, merciful Love onto all others I place on their path. I have patience with you so that you can have patience with others. I place My Own patient, merciful, forgiving Love _in_ you so that you can allow _My_ patient, forgiving, merciful, faithful Love to flow out onto others. Your weakness and sin offered to Me on the Cross is the source of healing and conversion—a passageway of life—for others. Rest with Me now—in My patient, wounded Heart always pouring forth great rivers of Love into the world. And I bless you ..."

Jesus also showed me later this answer to my question:

When I am cold, I like to hold a warm cup in my hands. It is the same when my heart is cold (it is always cold when I am alone) and so I must always hold Jesus' Heart—hot with the fire of His Love to warm me. When there are people with hearts so frozen in sin and they don't want to take Jesus' warm drink of Love from me, I can hold His Heart and simply stand close to them and eventually their frozen hearts will begin to melt.

Jesus was so patient in His Love on the Cross—and He never gave up hope. Even on the Cross He trusted in His Father, and when the time came for Him to die, He entrusted even His death into His Father's hands. He is an example for all missionaries—for we are called to hope in the darkness, trust when we feel abandoned and always be faithful in the hope of eternal life. When we remember Jesus' Own patient suffering on the Cross for our sins, it is much easier to remain patient with those who seem to be so lost in darkness and sin. Moses only had to hit a rock once and water came flowing out. And so, a heart hardened by sin and

suffering only needs one drop of Jesus' blood in order to break open. And yet although Jesus does convert some people in such miraculous ways, more often than not He desires to teach us His patient love from the Cross and so He allows us to be blind to the effects of our Love so that we will continue to be faithful in Love. A drop of water on a rock eventually can break a rock in half. And so, we must remember that a drop of Jesus' Love, continually pouring upon a broken or hardened soul, can and will eventually break it open to see His Love and Light.

Chapter 7

"Now in the place where Jesus was crucified there was a Garden…"

It is written in the Gospel of John that *'in the place where Jesus was crucified there was a garden…'* (John 19:41). It is a very interesting point of contemplation that in the midst of the horrors of Calvary there was a garden with flowers and new life. This hidden beauty in the midst of the passion of Jesus is something that often escapes people's notice, but it is a great symbol with a deep meaning. The fact that a beautiful garden existed where Jesus was crucified reminds us that in the midst of the Cross, darkness and suffering of Jesus' Passion, the beauty of Jesus' Love and flowers of new life were pouring forth from such horror. God was with Jesus and among His people pouring out His mercy and Love, even if most did not recognize Him at that moment. In the same way in our lives, when we meet the Cross, we can be tempted to focus solely on its horror. But God calls us to remember that in the place where we are crucified there also is a garden. He is present with us, pouring out His love, and striving to place new life even in the

midst of the most difficult situations.

This was a reality that I encountered deeply in Russia. The lives of every person I met seemed to be horrifically crucified—and yet I was called to draw their attention to the 'garden' surrounding them. I was called to show them God's Love with them, and His hope of eternal life. I was called to find His great Love and beauty in the most simple of things, just so that I could offer (both my) and their hearts hope. I remember on a few occasions craving beauty so deeply, for the city in which I was living was desperately ugly—grey concrete buildings, dirt, brokenness, and abandon. I walked around the city for an hour searching for 'beauty' until I finally found some weeds growing through the cracks in some broken concrete somewhere. I picked these 'flowers' and brought them home and put them in an oversized glass of water to present to sister when she returned home later that evening. It took lots of work, but it always was possible to find beauty in such little things. Other times, I marveled at how beautifully God created the pigeons (which at any other time I would have considered ugly and a nuisance) coloring each of their feathers with a little different color. Sometimes, the 'beauty' I would find would be in the tasty honey I would add to my cup of tea in the evening, fresh from a babuska's beehive. I would search to find signs of God's Love around me, and then strive to show these to those I served, who had lost faith that He loved or cared for them anymore. More than anything, I strove to keep Jesus' Love as a bright light in my heart. In remembering His promise of heaven and His deep presence of Love for me on earth in the Eucharist, the exterior trials I met lost

the heaviness of importance. In focusing on His fathomless Love, I
was able to diminish the 'great problems' we encountered in life
into simple splinters of inconvenience. In the Spring of 2003, I
wrote a letter about one example of being able to find such deep
gratitude in the midst of suffering. The following is an excerpt of
something I later wrote about the experience, as well as the letter
itself:

Living in Kansk in general was difficult because it was such
a depressing, ugly, broken, dirty place—as well as the great
waves of problems and hopelessness of the people there. Yet I
tried to find real joy in my life there. I reflected about how Jesus
left heaven—a place of perfection and beauty and Love—to

come to earth to save us. And the least I could do is leave the comfortability of America and of Krasnoyarsk in many ways, to come to Kansk and be a tool of God's Love for the people there. Jesus gave me so many graces in the few months that I lived in Kansk, I do not even know how to begin to describe them. Our moving to Kansk coincided with the beginning of Lent, and so our suffering there was a very appropriate and helpful reflection on the sufferings of Jesus. I wrote to someone describing my heart in the midst of all of this:

...I wanted to write to you about my heart. This is such a rich and mysterious time for me- moving to Kansk and being in Lent. I am so at peace in this- the will of my Father. I could never have imagined the great riches He is giving me—riches both of the Cross, as well as of grace and His Love. He is especially opening up to me His Eucharistic Heart's Crucified Love- as my Human Husband, and as My Savior Lord. He told me that He wanted this time to especially be with Him in the Eucharist. And although Kansk is a desert in so many ways, I feel like I am in Paradise (Heaven). Yes, it is difficult to even buy simple groceries here. Nothing is organized. We have had problems with the phone, lights, computer, water, and registering here already. The interior life of the people is very shallow. I could go on and on...Sister is really lonely. Father is lonelier. But, although all of these exterior things are a mess, Jesus has given us HIMSELF. We have Jesus, exposed in the monstrance for adoration, 24 hours a day IN MY HOME!! I have lived with the Blessed Sacrament before, but I have never lived with perpetual adoration. It is absolutely amazing. Every time something broke in the last two weeks, or something did not work, I could go in the chapel and it was all 'okay,' nothing mattered because I had Jesus. My Beloved Jesus' Eucharistic Heart was open, on the Cross, before me. I have been so filled by His tender, strong Love—nothing else matters. All I have here is Him. But that is all I need. I'm not eating for Lent. But He is my food. I sleep little—but He is my sleep. His Heart is my Home. He is my only friend, my only confessor; He was my only spiritual director…and I had to trust, and He was faithful. Fasting does not seem like a sacrifice (physically it does, but spiritually it is a Feast)! Not eating frees me to feast on His Love, His Eucharistic Crucified Love! He is so much closer to

me at this time…He fills and fills and fills me, even when I don't feel Him, don't see Him. He is with me in my darkness—because it is truly His darkness.

In the time of my greatest difficulties—living basically alone in Kansk the final Spring of 2003—Jesus continued to open up the mystery of His beauty in the midst of the Cross. During this time, He helped me to write a spiritual teaching on finding His great beauty and love in the midst of the darkness. The truths He shared with me in this work was the great 'garden of love' He gave to me in the midst of my little crucifixion. By helping me to focus on His Heart, His suffering, His hope and gift of salvation to all mankind, I was able to easily pass through the trials simply by trusting Him and surrendering to Him in Fiat. It is amazing what a powerful tool Love can be in such trials. But as He lit my heart afire with His Love, this Love carried me through the last few months I spent in Siberia and even further as I left this country and continued on where He called me to come. The spiritual lessons and gifts Jesus gave to me in this time is compiled in the book entitled, *Out of the Darkness.* This book has been published and is available every-where.

Chapter 8

"In the end, My Immaculate Heart will triumph!"
(Our Lady in Fatima—July 13, 1917)

I could not end a book about missionary life in Russia without including a chapter about Our Lady's promise in Fatima that after all was said and done, **in the end Her Immaculate Heart would triumph in the world *through Russia.*** Let's look directly at Her words containing both a prophesy and a promise:

The three children of Fatima—Lucia, Francisco, and Jacinta—said that in the apparition of Our Lady on July 13, 1917, the Virgin said to them:

"I shall come to ask for the Consecration of Russia to my Immaculate Heart. If people attend to my requests, Russia will be converted and the world will have peace."

Later during the July apparition, Our Lady promised the children that, in October, she would identify herself and perform a miracle so that all might see and believe.

She also gave the children a secret, which included a vision of hell that caused Lucia to cry out. Afterward, the Lady said:

"You have seen hell where the souls of poor sinners go. To save them, __God wishes to establish in the world devotion to my Immaculate Heart.__ If what I say to you is done, many souls will be saved and there will be peace. The war is going to end; but if people do not cease offending God, a worse one will break out during the pontificate of Pius XI. When you see a night illumined by an unknown light, know that this is the great sign given you by God that he is about to punish the world for its crimes, by means of war, famine, and persecutions of the Church and of the Holy Father.

"To prevent this, **I shall come to ask for the consecration of Russia to my Immaculate Heart, and the Communion of Reparation on the First Saturdays. If my requests are heeded, Russia will be converted, and there will be peace; if not, she will spread her errors throughout the world, causing wars and persecutions of the Church. The good will be martyred, the Holy Father will have much to suffer, various nations will be annihilated. __In the end, my Immaculate Heart will triumph. The Holy Father will consecrate Russia to me, and she will be converted, and a period of peace will be granted to the world...__** *Do not tell this to anybody."*

As you see from the preceding chapters of this book, Our Lady's prophecy of Russia's spread of her errors throughout the world and the subsequent suffering caused by this can clearly be seen to have come true. And yet, the message of Fatima and the story of Russia thankfully does not end there. Instead, it ends with hope. And this hope is for the conversion of Russia and the Triumph of the Immaculate Heart of Mary in the world through Russia, culminating in an era of peace. This hope that Our Lady ignites in our hearts through Her words of promise in Fatima is something that I witnessed daily in reality both in the years I served Russia in the missions, as well as in the following years as I stayed in contact with many faithful souls living there.

"In the place where Jesus was crucified there was a garden..." and in the place where Jesus has been crucified among His people in Russia, there is a garden of the Holy Spirit's flowers and fruits living the hearts of Our Lady's beloved people. The Triumph of the Immaculate Heart in Russia is beginning now, today, in the living hearts of the babushkas who light a candle before an icon of Our Lady or Our Lord in the corner of their living rooms each morning as they say their prayers. It is growing in the hearts of the newly baptized children being fed by the missionary love of the priests, sisters, and lay people who have dedicated their lives to nurturing the faith among the remnants of the Church still present there. And this era of peace spoken of by Our Lady is already a reality to God—Our Father Who always fulfills His Promises... it is already done from the eternal perspective... we simply wait for His plan to unfold in time on this side of eternity.

Each Hail Mary prayed on our rosaries offered for 'the conversion of Russia and the Triumph of the Immaculate Heart' plants peace in a land watered by so many martyrs' blood that it is called the Red Land... *"The blood of martyrs is the seed of faith"* and so the millions upon millions of martyred Christians over the

years in Russia united with the grace of Our Immaculate Mother's tears crying out for conversion of heart and peace together plead for Russia's conversion at the Throne of God in Heaven. It is through these martyrs' blood—as well as the white martyrdom of so many faithful—united to our own little suffering prayers for Russia—finding communion with each other on the Cross (our 'Common Thread')—that will eventually win the grace for Our Lady's Promise to come true. Her Immaculate Heart will triumph because of the faithful prayer and fasting of Her children offered in union with Her Son's Passion as He bled on the Cross in order for

Russia to be clean and pure. The Resurrection of Christ's Love will win in the world because His people will have chosen to remain faithful to His Passion and have loved with Him so fiercely that their hearts are carried into Eternity even while still their feet are on earth. Love will be won through this heroic sort of prayer and sacrifice. And the fruit of this Love will be seen all over the earth. In Our Lady of Fatima's message on June 13, 1917, She said,

"[Jesus] wishes to establish devotion to my Immaculate Heart in the world. I promise salvation to those who embrace it; and these souls will be beloved of God like flowers arranged by me to adorn His throne." May our prayer and fasting for Russia and with Russia for the world continually ascend to the heavens as perfumed flowers around the throne of the Lamb. Amen.

For More on Mary Kloska

For more information about Mary Kloska's vocation, books, icons (Artist Shop), music, podcasts, prayer ministry or to become a monthly donor to support her missionary work, please see:

www.marykloskafiat.com

Blog: http://fiatlove.blogspot.com

Books:

The Holiness of Womanhood:
https://enroutebooksandmedia.com/holinessofwomanhood/

Out of the Darkness
https://enroutebooksandmedia.com/outofthedarkness/

In Our Lady's Shadow: The Spirituality of Praying for Priests
https://enroutebooksandmedia.com/shadow/

La Santidad de La Mujer
https://enroutebooksandmedia.com/lasantidaddelamujer/

Swietosc Kobiecosci
https://enroutebooksandmedia.com/swietosckobiecosci/

Z Ciemnosci
https://enroutebooksandmedia.com/z-ciemnosci/

Radio
Podcasts: https://wcatradio.com/heartoffiatcrucifiedlove/

YouTube VIDEO Podcasts
Playlist: http://www.tinyurl.com/marykloska

Artist Shop (Icon prints and other items for sale): http://marykloskafiat.threadless.com

Music CD "FIAT" is also available on all music platforms.

Patreon: www.patreon.com/marykloskafiat

Fatima Prayers

1) The Fatima Prayer (Decade Prayer)

O my Jesus, forgive us our sins, save us from the fires of hell, lead all souls to Heaven, especially those most in need of Thy mercy. Amen.

Mary told the children that people should add this prayer to the end of each decade of the Rosary.

2) The Pardon Prayer

My God, I believe, I adore, I hope and I love Thee. I beg pardon for all those that do not believe, do not adore, do not hope and do not love Thee. Amen.

This prayer was given to the children by the Angel of Peace that visited them in 1916, the year before Mary appeared to them.

3) The Angel's Prayer

O Most Holy Trinity, Father, Son and Holy Ghost, I adore Thee profoundly. I offer Thee the most precious Body, Blood, Soul and Divinity of Jesus Christ present in all the tabernacles of the world, in reparation for the outrages, sacrileges and indifferences by which He is offended. By the infinite merits of the Sacred Heart of Jesus and the Immaculate Heart of Mary I beg the conversion of poor sinners. Amen.

*This is another prayer given to them by the Angel of
Peace. There was a Eucharistic host and chalice suspended in
the air, and the angel led them in kneeling before it and
praying this prayer.*

4) The Eucharistic Prayer

**Most Holy Trinity, I adore Thee! My God, my God, I
love Thee in the Most Blessed Sacrament. Amen.**

*When Mary appeared to the children for the first time on
May 13, 1917, she said, "You will have much to suffer, but
the grace of God will be your comfort." According to Sr.
Lucia, a bright light shone all around them, and without
thinking about it, they all started reciting this prayer.*

5) The Sacrifice Prayer

**O Jesus, it is for the love of Thee, in reparation for the
offenses committed against the Immaculate Heart of
Mary, and for the conversion of poor sinners [that I do
this]. Amen.**

*Mary gave the children this prayer, as well as the Fatima
Prayer/Decade Prayer, on June 13th, 1917. The prayer is
meant to be recited when you are offering up suffering to
God.*

"Stained-glass window in Corpus Christi, TX of Mary
helping to found the SOLT Russian Mission"